More Praise for *Peace First*

"Through *Peace First* Uri Savir proves that he is one of the chief stewards of the temple of peace. He continues to fulfill his duties with great perseverance, and he dedicates his intellectual life to finding solutions to conflict and unearthing the origins of the idea that tyrannizes him—peace."

— Abu Ala (Ahmed Qurei), former Prime Minister of the Palestinian Authority

"When Uri Savir says it is time to modernize our approach to peace, he is surely correct. One thing is for sure: leaders trying to resolve historic conflicts need help from within and from without to marshal the wherewithal to confront both history and mythology. Uri Savir is certainly doing his part to help."

— Ambassador Dennis Ross, Ziegler Distinguished Fellow, The Washington Institute for Near East Policy, and author of *Statecraft: And How to Restore America's Standing in the World*

"In this book, Savir outlines a radical and innovative approach to the peace process in an effort to change the paradigm and move peace forward. In an era where new ideas seem in short supply, Savir soldiers on, with creativity, integrity, and a never-ending commitment to bring much-needed peace to the region."

— Dr. Marwan Muasher, Senior Vice President, External Affairs, World Bank, and author of *The Arab Center: The Promise of Moderation*

"This is a wise and compelling reassessment of approaches to negotiating the resolution of conflicts in an ever-more-complex international environment. Uri Savir's emphasis on combining the global with the local makes a unique contribution to the challenge of peacemaking in the Middle East and beyond."

— Martin Indyk, Director, Saban Center for Middle East Policy, The Brookings Institution, and former U.S. Ambassador to Israel

"A thoughtful examination of the challenge of peacemaking in a world where shifting parameters—the rise of nonstate actors, the increase in international terrorism, the advance of military technology, the growing rift between the Western and Islamic societies, the rise of extremism—have created a new strategic paradigm. A serious and insightful case for a new approach to conflict resolution."

— Javier Solana, High Representative for the Common Foreign and Security Policy, European Union

"Israel's pre-eminent diplomat, Ambassador Uri Savir, has authored a highly innovative perspective on how international state-to-state diplomacy has to be supplemented by a people-to-people approach. The grand master of Middle East peace negotiations has again proved his groundbreaking diplomatic stature through a city-to-city angle in our age of urbanization."

    – Terje Rød-Larsen, President, International Peace Institute

"Drawing from his rich personal experience, Savir has the courage and the vision to explain why narrow, conventional approaches to security are bound to prove insufficient in the 21st century. I particularly welcome Savir's proposal for a Pax Mediterraneo that embraces everybody in the region, without exception—a task that seems to me more urgent than ever."

    – Miguel Moratinos, Minister of Foreign Affairs and Cooperation, Spain

"In Essaouira-Mogador, my tiny hometown, I was educated by my rabbis and teachers to first take care of my neighbors. Today my neighbor is Palestinian... By fighting for a just and decent peace between Palestine and Israel I am fighting for my own heritage...On this frustrating but illuminating road to peace Uri was one of the very few colleagues and dear friends who paved the way."

    – Andre Azoulay, Counselor to the King of Morocco

"A timely and valuable book...Uri gives us a rich menu of new and creative models for peacemaking. A must-read for scholars and negotiators involved in vital issues of peacemaking."

    – Toni G. Verstandig, Senior Policy Advisor, Center for Middle East Peace and Economic Cooperation, and Executive Director, Aspen Institute's Middle East Strategy Group

"Uri Savir's book *Peace First* is a creative and courageous new model for peacemaking in our world. The book has depth and compelling analysis—a must-read for anyone concerned with bringing peace to the countless war-torn regions across the globe."

    – Quincy Jones, music impresario and founder of the Quincy Jones Listen Up Foundation

"Uri Savir's commitment and expert knowledge can never be questioned. In *Peace First* he has discovered the clearest and most possible path toward peace. It should be required reading for every diplomat."

    – Kathleen Turner, actress

"Peace is the process that begins in the individual heart. It is a need to live without grief, despair, or expectation. A desire to give with release. It is the ecstasy of tranquility."

    – Sharon Stone, actress

PEACE FIRST

PEACE FIRST

A New Model to End War

URI SAVIR

Berrett–Koehler Publishers, Inc.
San Francisco
a BK Currents book

Berrett-Koehler Publishers, Inc.
235 Montgomery Street, Suite 650, San Francisco, CA 94104-2916
Tel: (415) 288-0260   Fax: (415) 362-2512   www.bkconnection.com

ORDERING INFORMATION

QUANTITY SALES. Special discounts are available on quantity purchases by corporations, associations, and others. For details, contact the "Special Sales Department" at the Berrett-Koehler address above.

INDIVIDUAL SALES. Berrett-Koehler publications are available through most bookstores. They can also be ordered directly from Berrett-Koehler:
Tel: (800) 929-2929; Fax: (802) 864-7626; www.bkconnection.com

ORDERS FOR COLLEGE TEXTBOOK/COURSE ADOPTION USE. Please contact Berrett-Koehler: Tel: (800) 929-2929; Fax: (802) 864-7626.

ORDERS BY U.S. TRADE BOOKSTORES AND WHOLESALERS. Please contact Ingram Publisher Services, Tel: (800) 509-4887; Fax: (800) 838-1149;
E-mail: customer.service@ingrampublisherservices.com; or visit www
.ingrampublisherservices.com/Ordering for details about electronic ordering.

Berrett-Koehler and the BK logo are registered trademarks of Berrett-Koehler Publishers, Inc.

Printed in the United States of America

Berrett-Koehler books are printed on long-lasting acid-free paper. When it is available, we choose paper that has been manufactured by environmentally responsible processes. These may include using trees grown in sustainable forests, incorporating recycled paper, minimizing chlorine in bleaching, or recycling the energy produced at the paper mill.

LIBRARY OF CONGRESS CATALOGING-IN-PUBLICATION DATA
Savir, Uri.
[Kodem shalom. English]
Peace first: a new model to end war / by Uri Savir.
    p.   cm.
Includes bibliographical references and index.
ISBN 978-1-57675-596-9 (hardcover: alk. paper)
1. Arab-Israeli conflict—1993—Peace.   I. Title.
DS119.76.S2813   2008
956.05—dc22

                                                        2008021305

First Edition

13 12 11 10 09 08   10 9 8 7 6 5 4 3 2 1
Project management, interior design, and composition by Scribe Typography. Copyediting by Manza Editorial. Proofreading by Manza Editorial and Don Roberts. Index by Stephanie Maher Palenque.

To my beloved Aliza.
May our grandchildren,
Lenny, Miki, Anouk, and Alon,
grow up in an Israel of peace.

CONTENTS

FOREWORD

by Shimon Peres

PEACE REFLECTS THE MOST FUNDAMENTAL RIGHT AND HUMAN desire—the right to life. Peace is the right of a parent to protect a child from poverty and conflict, and peace is the profound social diktat that a man must put down his gun. And although peace should therefore be considered the natural state of affairs, war seems to be the only constant in our history. Peace is the time between wars, and war is *legitimately* employed to pursue a society's interests.

Technology and the free market economy have transformed the world into a global village, and the phenomenon of globalization has become the pivotal element that should create world peace. Yet the unprecedented wealth generated by the forces of globalization has been amassed by the developed world rather than substantively dispersed to the poor and developing nations so desperate to reap its fruits. While the champions and beneficiaries of globalization continue to accumulate wealth, know-how, and power; to reach unparalleled levels of education, communication, and quality of life; and to create a megaculture as a byproduct, the other half still lives differently. The developing world remains impoverished and disease-stricken, and many of these countries exist to sustain conflict.

The ever-increasing gap between the developing and developed worlds is engendering a new conflict; the impoverished now threaten world peace. The union of poverty, fundamentalist ideologies, and weapons of mass destruction is a devastating hybrid that has planted its roots in the fertile lands of frustrated and estranged constituencies.

In such conditions, creating and sustaining peace is an arduous task. And in this sense, the peace-desiring world does not face an enemy in the traditional sense. Rather, we must confront the issues of the day: poverty, extremism, terrorism, dissemination of unconventional weaponry, pollution, and cultural estrangement.

Globalization has intensified these challenges. The power of the nation-state is in steady decline as it becomes decentralized, moving from central governments to other institutions. Capital has moved from the public sector to the private sector, promoting social values has become the task of nongovernmental organizations, and even war is less an act of state than an operation of violent terrorist groups.

In this state of the world, peacemaking must be reformed. A new coalition of forces must pave the way to a citizens' peace, involving a complex puzzle of participants and interactions to ensure the sustainability of peace.

In this book, Uri Savir has endeavored to confront these important challenges by offering a solution to the peacemaking puzzle that is courageous, innovative, and based on his extensive experience as a peacemaker. This groundbreaking book presents readers with a fresh approach to the most important challenge of this century—making peace. It will no doubt contribute to the necessary debate on the critical question of how to make peace in our era.

FOREWORD

by Dennis Ross

FOR SOMEONE WHO WORKED CLOSELY WITH URI SAVIR DUR-
ing Israel's negotiations with its neighbors in the 1990s, it comes
as no surprise to me that he would write a book on why we must
revolutionize the way we approach peacemaking and how we can
do so. I say this because, as a negotiator, Uri Savir brought not just
skills, creativity, and insight to the task; he brought empathy and
compassion as well.

Uri, first and foremost, is an Israeli patriot. But he is also a
humanist. He believed that peace with Israel's neighbors was in
Israel's national interests. He believed in a peace of mutual interest, not a peace of surrender. He believed in a peace of openness,
with reconciliation and cooperation, not a cold peace of isolation
and separation. He believed in a peace in which each side could
gain, not one in which he would necessarily get the better of his
counterparts. (That did not mean he would let them get the better
of him or his country.)

Throughout the Oslo process, Uri saw peace as most enduring
if it reflected the self-interest of both sides. Peace could not be a
favor that one side did for the other, nor could it represent a sacrifice of something so basic that one side could not sustain or fulfill
the commitments made.

Uri was not sentimental in his negotiating, but he worked hard
to understand the needs of the other side—whether it was in his
negotiations with the Palestinians or with the Syrians. For him this
was not a sacrifice but a hardheaded way of achieving what Israel
needed; the more he could demonstrate that he understood what
the other side needed (and could explain it), the more he could

explain what he needed on his side to be responsive. He took a long view of peacemaking, always having a strategic vision of where he wanted to go and not letting short-term tactics undercut his longer-term direction.

For someone who labored so hard to make Oslo work, only to see it come crashing down years after his efforts from 1993 to 1996, it is not surprising that Uri would ask questions about its demise and try to learn the lessons that might be applied to peacemaking today. Many such questions are embedded in this book, and they help explain the model for peacemaking that he proposes. For example:

- Why was it so hard to produce a peacemaking process that gained public support and acceptance of the peace narrative?

- Why did the opponents of peace, especially those who used violence and terror, always seem to have the upper hand?

- Why was such a narrow approach taken to peacemaking, putting a premium on security but not on building civil society or the economic underpinnings of peace?

- Why wasn't the region and the international community enlisted to more effectively support the peacemaking process?

- Why weren't the donor countries and their private sectors called on to invest in joint economic developments between Israelis and Palestinians, not only to produce economic peace dividends but also to foster a new psychology of cooperation and joint ventures?

- Why wasn't more done to connect the two societies and the youths in those societies? Peace, after all, is made between peoples and not just among national abstractions.

- Why was the strategy for implementation of agreements so limited and always so vulnerable to being frustrated?

Although I may be posing these questions more explicitly than

Uri does in the book, he offers answers to these and other questions to help explain why Oslo and other such efforts to resolve historic conflicts have not succeeded. Uri presents not just a new model for peacemaking but also a strategy for pursuing it.

He calls for a "participatory peace" in which citizens are integrated into the effort. He speaks of the need for "glocalization," in which the new reality of decentralization from national governments is recognized and in which cities across national boundaries and around the globe are enlisted to work together on common problems. He refers to the need to develop a "peace ecology" in which the culture of peace and cooperation is nurtured, as opposed to the traditional mind-set that sees peace agreements as more formal and geared only toward the cessation of conflict. He focuses on "peace building" not just peacemaking, arguing that building peace through connecting societies, promoting common economic ventures, and creating sports and cultural programs among the youth will do more to make peace a reality than simply talking about it.

Finally, Uri calls for "creative diplomacy," the need to bring many different local, regional, and international actors into the process. In addition, he offers a new tutorial on how best to negotiate. This is a book that offers not only a new taxonomy of terms for peacemaking but also a new theory about what is required and how to do it.

Uri is not motivated only by the failures of the past. Instead, he is deeply troubled by the new threats he sees emerging in a globalized world in which there is an enormous underclass left out and left behind—a reality that fosters anger, alienation, and frustration and that broadens the appeal of those ready to engage in apocalyptic terrorist acts. Ongoing historic conflicts also create a fertile breeding ground for suicidal attackers, and the potential marriage of the worst weapons with actors ready to commit unspeakable acts of terror on a mass scale creates very plausible doomsday scenarios. Uri starts the book with such a scenario in mind, to explain why we must take a revolutionary approach to peacemaking.

Uri is focused not only on resolving historic conflicts but also on thinking about how we use the tools of globalization—the new means of connecting citizens and the new focal points of power, such as mayors less hamstrung by bureaucracies—to overcome the international divides that create a context for conflict.

Not every reader of this book will buy the argument that security can be downplayed relative to the need to promote cooperation. But this is not a book that requires acceptance of every detailed proposal. Instead, it is a book that requires us to stretch our minds and decide that it is time to modernize our approach to peacemaking—just as war has always commanded new technologies, new innovations, and new doctrines.

When Uri Savir says it is time to modernize our approach to peace, he is surely correct. When he tells us we need a peace barometer or a new talisman for implementation of peace agreements, we ought to listen. His book charts a new course for peacemaking that is desperately needed. For someone who has waged the battle for peace along with him, I share the view that we need a revolutionary approach to peacemaking. One thing is for sure: leaders trying to resolve historic conflicts need help from within and from without to marshal the wherewithal to confront both history and mythology. Uri Savir is certainly doing his part to help.

Making Peace in a World at War

THIS BOOK IS THE RESULT OF MY PERSONAL AND NATIONAL distress.

From a personal perspective, I wrote this book while recovering from a severe stroke. It is believed that distress sharpens one's thinking; this was certainly my experience. In writing this book I was reconnecting with life. For me, there is no stronger expression of life than yearning for peace.

In national terms, this book emerged from a place of disappointment regarding the implementation of the Oslo Accords. As chief negotiator for Israel, I was profoundly invested in the process. Yet, despite the agreement's historical achievements, both Israelis and Palestinians are still trapped within a culture of conflict; the region remains pitted with emotional and practical obstacles to peace.

This distress, I believe, is not mine alone; the struggle of Israel and Palestine is symptomatic of the struggles in the world at large. In 1945, there were fewer than 20 high- and medium-intensity conflicts worldwide. By 2007, that number had risen to one hundred thirty, including twenty-five "severe crises" and six wars characterized by massive amounts of violence, according to the Heidelberg Institute for International Conflict Research's Conflict Barometer 2007.[1] A vast majority of the more than one hundred partial and full peace agreements signed over the past two decades[2] have endured severe sustainability issues or have simply fallen apart. And despite the fourteen Nobel Peace Prizes that have drifted through the Middle East, South Africa, and Northern Ireland,[3] not one region fully enjoys the true fruits of peace.

In this light, our future as a species looks dim indeed. But I believe our current path is defined less by the inevitabilities of human nature and more by structural failures in the way we make peace. Consider: Little in today's world is more progressive than modern warfare. High-tech intelligence-collection methods, laser-guided missiles that surgically destroy targets, vision-enhancing technology that enables night missions, and other devices straight out of science fiction offer warmakers a buffet of enticing tools that were not available during the World Wars, let alone during nineteenth-century battles.

On the other hand, few things are more archaic than today's peacemaking strategies. Contemporary peace processes and treaties mirror those of the past; our strategies have been left stranded somewhere in the nineteenth century. I do not mean that modern technologies are not manifest in current peace efforts; computers and the Internet are integral parts of planning and negotiations. But while the social, political, and economic elements of societies have evolved to encompass globalization, modern technology, and communication, peacemaking as a strategy has remained stagnant.

The inability of peacemakers to cope with progress is linked to the traditional character of peacemaking. Throughout human history, peacemaking has served to unravel the historical knots of military issues, security, and the distribution of power and physical assets, such as land and natural resources in colonial times; rarely has it established the groundwork for a future peace. The fact that many of today's peacemakers are yesterday's warmakers—or worse, simultaneously operate as warmakers—makes force seem like a realistic way to "keep the peace." Thus, strategic security considerations maintain their status as the centerpiece in the transition from violence to nonviolence, and peace is merely perceived as the time between wars.

This cannot continue. As long as we view peace as simply one point on a continuum of war, we will never create real, lasting peace. We are still convinced that behind every conflict lies a culprit—but the enemy is not the Other; it is our own archaic definition of what peace is and how to achieve it.

We stand today at a crossroads. In one direction lie conflict, mistrust, and hostility. If we continue down this path, as we have done for ages, the following scenario is not unlikely: A chemical terror attack on a Tel Aviv subway sparks a series of targeted bombings against the Iranian Embassy in Beirut. As Lebanese emergency personnel clear away the wreckage, hundreds of thousands of people demonstrate in front of the US Delegation in Tehran. Iran's president threatens to attack US military forces stationed on the Golan Heights, and the US president announces a high alert situation and threatens the use of nuclear weapons against Iran. CNN broadcasts a special appeal by religious leaders to prevent an apocalypse; the United Nations deems the world on the verge of disaster.

But there is another path, one that leads to a future of cooperation and understanding. This book points the way toward this new direction—a revolutionary model for modern peace. It reflects the changes wrought by globalization, including the erosion of the nation-state's power and the consolidation of power within the private sector and civil society. It lays out a road map for transition from an outmoded definition of peacemaking to a modern one, from an exclusive to a participatory process, from a culture of war to a culture of peace.

The concepts in this book have been distilled from a lifetime of experience. My professional life has been dedicated to peacemaking and peacebuilding; I am a man obsessed. I have endeavored to *make* peace with the Palestinians as Israel's chief negotiator of the Oslo Accords, and with Syria and Jordan as the head of our foreign ministry. I also have attempted to *build* peace through the establishment of two nongovernmental organizations (NGOs), the Peres Center for Peace in Tel Aviv and the Glocal Forum in Rome. These NGOs have supported activities that foster cooperation between enemies and former enemies in the Middle East; in the African nations of Ethiopia, Eritrea, Rwanda, and Sierra Leone; in the European regions of Northern Ireland and the former Yugoslavia; and in the Asian nations of Afghanistan, India, and Pakistan.

Over the years, I have received invaluable guidance from individuals who have combined passion and practicality in their tireless efforts toward peace: my late father, Leo Savir, who was a brilliant and sophisticated soldier for peace; my political father, Shimon Peres, a great visionary, an unmatched statesman, and a man of the world; my wife, Aliza, who carries the torch of peace and possesses a wonderful gift of abstraction; my daughter, Maya, with her most pure values; and many friends and colleagues, including Amnon Lipkin-Shahak, a man of integrity; Yossi Ginossar, who is not with us today but who pushed hard for peace and reconciled defense with human understanding; my partner at the Peres Center for Peace, Dr. Ron Pundak, who is a significant individual in the realm of civil society; Abu Ala, my Palestinian counterpart, who, while he sat on the other side of the table, taught me a great deal through his wisdom and creative peacemaking; James Wolfensohn, the former president of the World Bank, a man of peace who understands better than anyone the link between economic development and peacemaking; Terje Rod-Larsen, the facilitator of the Oslo process and a man of true peace and humanity; Dennis Ross, the most committed and wise peace mediator in the US administration; and many more.

Influenced by these and other individuals, my approach to peacemaking is based on an ideological framework that places equality between human beings at its pinnacle; this is an equality that cannot exist in war. I am not a pacifist. I know that there are just and ultimately beneficial wars, but I believe these wars are limited. War is not heaven-sent but man-made; it is a product of human nature and is thus shaped by human desires, such as the preservation of identity, greater control over territory, and the expansion of resources. Paradoxically, many feel comfort in the culture of conflict—the comfort of the status quo.

However, I believe the greatest desire of a human being is the desire to survive. This desire must be translated into the most basic right, to live and let live—in other words, the right to peace. From this perspective, peace is not only a strategic objective but also a fulfillment of our most fundamental human desires.

Both the United States and Israel have recently learned firsthand the difficulty of fighting wars against guerilla forces and against terror. It is perhaps the first time in history that developing countries or independent groups have the ability to endanger world peace. In an era in which the weak have become strong—based on fertile grounds of fundamentalism, fed by poverty, religious extremism, and the proliferation of unconventional weapons—peace has become the most necessary and useful wall of defense. Military power in the traditional sense no longer deters rogue armies, as the United States has learned from Vietnam, Afghanistan, and Iraq. Making peace has not become easier, but it is an imperative.

The US administration emphasizes political reform and democratization as conditions for peace. The importance of democracy is indisputable, but it is not enough to ensure either short- or long-term peace. It is true that democracies have rarely waged war against each other, but it is also true that democracies *have* waged wars, some necessary, some less so. Furthermore, in situations of social and economic frustration, pro-peace forces can be outvoted in democratic societies; free elections can bring fundamentalist and extremist regimes to power—just look at the 2006 parliamentary elections in the Palestinian Authority.

Iraq is another case in point. Despite massive military attacks and the imposition of "democracy," the United States has been unable to bring peace to the region. The insurgency—acting in opposition to coalition forces, their Iraqi partners, and innocent civilians—has not diminished. Iraq without Saddam Hussein is further from peace than was ever anticipated. The combination of frustration, poverty, and hostility, married with terrorism and the upsurge of nonconventional weapons, has rendered the traditional balance of power irrelevant. Iran is yet another prime example of this power inversion.

Another theory popular among global actors suggests that

economy is the key to peace; with regional and local economic development at stake, both sides in a conflict will have too much to lose and will therefore opt for peace. Theoretically, this is true. In reality, however, economic development is an important but not a sufficient—or even a realistic—condition for peace. Conflict states, such as those in the Middle East and Africa, often experience massive socioeconomic gaps as a result of inflated defense budgets.[4] Poor populations suffer the most under these conditions, as military spending takes priority over educational and health development. As a result, the poor understandably view peace as the revolution of the rich, and they rebel against it. Thus, regional economic development before peace is extremely difficult—virtually impossible. Legal and psychological barriers often prevent cooperation, and instability prevents external investment, especially by the private sector, which does not tend to take risks in unstable regions.

Besides, time is precious; peace cannot simply be the domino effect of other processes—it must come first. The international community must make an astute and innovative shift in its approach to peace: peacemaking must be modernized to reflect the new world order and should be set as the first priority on the international agenda.

To begin, we must recognize that governments, within the current framework of the international system, will not be the champions of peace. Governments may facilitate peace, but first the international system must be reformed to create a peacemaking coalition in which governments will serve as but one of the major players. Even then, there are limits to the argument that the new world governance of globalism and regionalism will resolve issues of war and peace.

On the contrary, peacemaking must be decentralized, and world citizens—through the medium of local governments and nongovernmental organizations—must be willing and able participants. Peace can thus become democratized, and a participatory process involving the hearts and minds of individuals can be ingrained within the international system. Peace must be engaged at the grassroots. It can never be sustained purely by a balance of power; it is sustainable only if a society wills it. This is crucial in conflict-laden regions, where the potential for violent opposition is inherent. Put simply, it is easier to democratize peace than to democratize autocratic societies.

After we change our approach to security and the distribution of power and assets during peacemaking, governments and societies will have to confront complex and urgent notions of stabilization from an alternative perspective. The motivation to *not* employ weapons is more crucial than a state's capacity to develop and use them; hence, the routine security element that is still considered the focal point in a transition from violence to peace has become less pertinent.

In essence, modern peace depends on the mobility that societies stand to gain from peace rather than on the power that emanates from the use of violence. Social, economic, and cultural attributes are critical to redirecting countries toward a culture of peace. Throughout this book, I focus on new and broader definitions of security, social mobility, the creation of a culture of peace, and integrative and cooperative regional economic development. Ultimately, I present a new model for peace leadership that deals with peace as both a means and an end—including the creation of a participatory political system and the necessary reform of the international peace support system.

Part 1 of this book analyzes the current problems with peace, identifying obsolete elements and structural weaknesses of traditional peace processes and treaties during the last century. Current peacemaking efforts are plagued by outdated perceptions and security dogmas that lack notions of social mobility, that bureaucratize the process, that represent a revolution of the elite, and that promote suspicion and hostility; these efforts must be modernized in light of the evolving international system. I also highlight the Oslo process in retrospect, because this is the peace process with which I was most involved and because it represents a mixed model of both outdated and modern peacemaking elements.

Part 2 introduces an innovative model for modern peace that opens the "closed doors" of most diplomatic encounters and invites all members of society to contribute to the creation of lasting peace. Although the suggestion might seem surprising coming from a veteran of secret diplomacy, experience has taught me that the modern house of peace must be built on the following four pillars: participatory peace and glocalization, peace ecology, peacebuilding, and creative diplomacy.

Participatory peace and glocalization integrates *local* agents into *global* issues. Current peacemaking involves narrow groups of leaders and diplomats—often the same people who lead war efforts in the first place. To achieve sustainable peace, we must decentralize the process and involve people from all segments of society. The ideals and goals of peaceful cooperation can be introduced by national governments, but local actors—city mayors, heads of local organizations, and members of civil society—will ensure their implementation. Cities can be linked by tourism, trade, youth projects, and more, creating a "glocal" web of entities invested in lasting peace.

Peace ecology involves a transition from a psychological and cultural environment of war to one of peace, based on common values, tolerance, and coexistence. Societies, like individuals, often define themselves by how they are different from others; during conflict, these differences become amplified and are used to justify aggression toward the enemy. By opening lines of communication and emphasizing commonalities rather than differences, those physical and psychological barriers can be dissolved. Media campaigns and cooperation between conflict groups are critical elements of infusing post-conflict societies with notions of human rights and equality.

Societies and governments act according to the dominant values and myths of the day, which is why peace ecology must address a society's beliefs and ideals at its roots. People must consciously move from a culture of war—defined by nationalistic values and hostility toward the enemy—to a culture of peace, in which coexistence with the former enemy is seen as beneficial. The shift can germinate both externally, through international and regional players, and internally, within the conflict area.

Peacebuilding focuses on cooperative activities and projects that build physical, financial, and social bridges between former enemies. Real peace is not merely the absence of war; it is the creation of links between adversaries where no links existed before. Cooperation in joint ventures generates more effective partnerships and cements common interests between former enemies. Projects such as infrastructure development in border cities, water- and energy-sharing programs, and the expansion of cross-border industries can narrow socioeconomic gaps between regions and thus diminish poverty-fueled frustrations. Youth and sport programs promote positive interactions between conflict groups. Overall, open borders introduce globalization and intersocietal cooperation in industries such as tourism, information technology, sports, and entertainment. Peacebuilding establishes cooperative development as a building block, rather than an afterthought, in a region's peace strategy.

Creative diplomacy has a simple goal: to make everyone feel that they've won. Current negotiations often seem like tug-of-wars, with each side pulling as hard as it can to "win ground" and make sure it doesn't "lose out" on important concessions. The term *compromise* has negative connotations, when in fact it should be considered a truly positive engagement. In creative diplomacy, the tug-of-war rope is dropped and peacemaking instead focuses on the positive developments *both sides* will experience with the cultivation of lasting peace. This kind of interaction requires innovation and flexibility to overcome stubbornness, biased interpretations of historical events, and aggressive security arrangements. Creative diplomacy deals with security more sophisticatedly, reconciling military and civilian needs.

These four pillars are naturally interrelated and are to some degree interdependent. I call them "pillars" because they are the foundation on which modern peace must rest.

Part 3 presents methods for incorporating these four essential pillars into a modern peace process. I lay out the conditions that have been proven to be conducive to peace and propose the planning of a new peace that involves analysis of public attitudes, innovation of negotiation and implementation techniques, and the creation of local, regional, and international peacemaking structures.

Part 4 integrates the concepts of parts 1 through 3 into a real, attainable peacemaking model for the Mediterranean region. This Pax Mediterraneo pertains to conflicts in Israel and Palestine, the Middle East, the former Yugoslavia, and Cyprus as well as to tensions between the northern and southern regions—southern Europe and northern Africa. As an extended case study, part 4 will be especially useful for students and practitioners of peace.

Finally, the conclusion outlines a new vision for the year 2020. I share the thoughts and hopes of some of humanity's greatest social and political figures, including Nelson Mandela, Shimon Peres, Mikhail Gorbachev, and others.

Peacemaking is about life and death. It demands that we honestly challenge our motives, values, and perceptions if we are to create and sustain real peace. The arguments in this book are based on empirical evidence from my extensive peacemaking experience as well as practical analysis from many peacemaking luminaries. Inherent in my subject matter is a Middle East bias. However, given the centrality of the Middle East conflict and the participation of virtually all major international players in the region, I do not believe that such a bias detracts from the global relevance of my proffered peacemaking model.

In fact, the Middle East faces the same critical battle as the rest of the world: the battle for peace in an environment full of obstacles, suspicion, and hostility. Just as there can be a "necessary war," so is there a "necessary peace." Our most brilliant minds must be directed toward such a battle—not peace at all costs, but a comprehensive, participatory peace that integrates the practical interests of all sides of the conflict and all parts of society. Such is the purpose of this book.

I am driven by both passion and pragmatism in my efforts toward a modern peacemaking model. The need for a new architecture of peace is clear, as are the consequences if we fail in our peacemaking efforts. When I consider the future of my four grandchildren, I wonder whether they will grow up in a culture of peace or in the throes of World War III. Will their generation experience headlines of hope or headlines of chemical attacks, nuclear threats, and widespread destruction?

The realization of either Armageddon or redemption depends on whether the world is able to create real, sustainable peace. The process of solving conflict and ending instability must begin in the endeavor for peace. Peace first.

PART I

The Challenge

Archaic Peace

CHAPTER ONE

Old-Fashioned Peacemaking

HISTORY IS BEING WRITTEN IN THE RED INK OF BLOOD AND not in the black ink of peace treaties.

For thousands of years, war has enabled countries and societies to conquer land, procure assets, and acquire power. As a result, any peace that follows from war has mostly focused on tangible achievements or failures, assets and power secured and squandered. The wise Chinese Communist leader Chou En-lai, paraphrasing Clausewitz, said, "All diplomacy is the continuation of war by other means."

The same can be said about peace. Peace treaties have traditionally declared an end to fighting; established formal, legally oriented relations; and included an inventory of assets, such as land, industrial resources, and prisoners of war, to be distributed upon the cessation of war—but not much more. Although such tangible acquisitions and losses have become less relevant in modern war, a model focused on security and assets is crystallized in the histories of most countries, whose peaceful reconciliation developed only after persistent struggles for influence, control, and colonies.

Peace represents a fundamental human freedom—the right to live. But peace, freedom, and democracy have been almost mutually exclusive throughout history. Even after democracy has permeated the international system, peace has continued to be a method to consolidate and distribute assets, territory, natural resources, and influence. When war was waged in the name of independence from colonial powers, such as the American Revolutionary War (1775–1783), some liberties and democratic elements resulted. However, even the US pursuit of peace by way of war discounted the interests and human rights of the defeated side. Furthermore, the spoils of war were mostly guaranteed to the state, the government, and the elite.

Paradoxically, war has become a more participatory process than peace. This contradiction stems from our historical understanding of peace as a strategic concept rather than a human right. Western peacemaking and peace treaties, both domestic and international, have evolved only minimally from "real estate" treaties into broader documents pursuing peace.

In this chapter, I will first dissect a handful of case studies from modern Western history to illustrate the evolution of peacemaking. I will then extract the core failures of Western peacemaking and explain them in light of recent peace treaties. We begin with the world's current great superpower, the United States.

As early as the nineteenth century, treaties such as those between the US government and the Indian tribes (for example, the 1805 Chickasaw Treaty) were essentially real estate treaties based on the ceding of territory, the relinquishment and acquisition of property, and financial recompense.[1] The Barbary Treaties (1786–1816) between the US authorities and the king of Algiers were similarly formatted as commercial agreements pertaining to the distribution of chattels, outlining conservative security arrangements alluding to the expectation of future wars, and establishing formal diplomatic relations, including the free expression of religion.[2]

Such modes of "peaceful settlement" also were reflected in European peace treaties during the "age of nation-states" (from the mid-eighteenth century through the Crimean War of 1854–1856), the Second Industrial Revolution (1870–1914), the unifications of Germany and Italy (1871), the Danish-Prussian War (1864), the Austro-Prussian War (1866), and the Franco-Prussian War (1870–1871). The aims of these wars defined the nature of the peace that followed: the conquering and consolidation of territory in the Crimean War, in which Russia endeavored to extend its control over various Ottoman provinces; and the maintaining of monarchies and the unification of territory, which was Otto von Bismarck's raison d'être. Although he was a master of diplomacy, Bismarck perceived peace as the amplification of German power and the acquisition of assets to strengthen coalitions.

Similarly, the Spanish-American War (1898) resulted in US control over former Spanish colonies in the Caribbean and Pacific. In a war of independence, Cuban rebels fought the Spanish while the US Congress passed joint resolutions proclaiming Cuba "free and independent." Spain broke off diplomatic relations with the United States, resulting in a declaration of war between the United States and Spain. The Treaty of Paris (1898) formally ended hostilities. The treaty gave the United States almost all of Spain's colonies and dealt with the relinquishment of Spanish property and associated rights—more like a property settlement following a divorce than a peace treaty. The First Amendment credo of equality and respect was not at all evident in this or in ensuing treaties between the United States and its former enemies.

Twentieth-century diplomacy begins prior to World War I (1914) and ends in 1990. Historian Eric Hobsbawm calls it a "century of extremism,"[3] which ran the gamut from fascism to communism, with commonalities characterizing both extremes. Additionally, a Eurocentric view was prevalent throughout this period; Europeans saw themselves as the center of the earth, not just physically but also culturally, believing that people on the periphery needed to be "acculturated" through imperialism.

Such arrogance was manifest in the Treaty of Versailles (1919),[4] which essentially served to guarantee assets, territories, and compensation—fundamental elements of imperial culture—and created a hegemonic narrative in which Germany was defeated and blamed. This defeat resulted in a sense of isolation and humiliation on the part of most Germans, whose sense of grievance was later exploited by Hitler in his quest for power.

Indeed, such a diktat can only survive temporarily. If a peace agreement is not reciprocal, providing both sides with an incentive for peace, it will not stand the test of time. The challenge of Versailles was to win the war and create a new international system so that all sides could live together; instead, the human instinct for total victory dominated. This was the ultimate mistake of the architects of Versailles, and it became the impetus for totalitarianism in Germany.

In retrospect, the lessons of Versailles—including the contrast between the New World, symbolized by a vigorous America emerging as a global power, and the old colonial European world weighed down by tradition and resistance to change—penetrated the global peace agenda only after World War II. Perhaps the most significant consequence of this war over the long term was the rebalancing of world power and the establishment of two spheres of influence. Britain, France, Germany, and Japan ceased to be great powers in the traditional military sense, leaving only the United States and the Soviet Union. The failures of Versailles prompted the United States to work with Europe against the Soviet Union; the United States recruited Germany and Japan into cooperation instead of threatening a reprisal.

This movement toward cooperation is reflected in the North Atlantic Treaty (1949),[5] which emphasizes freedom of the individual, democracy, rule of law, and the protection of the heritage of the West. The agreement, which formed the North Atlantic Treaty Organization (NATO), highlights a liberal, legal view with respect to stability and prosperity in the North Atlantic, not a totalitarian view of an inclusive peace. The NATO agreement was supported by the Marshall Plan (1947), an initiative of US Secretary of State George Marshall, which offered Europe up to $20 billion for relief if the European nations cooperated to create a reasonable aid plan.[6] The nations were obliged to work together and to act as a single economic unit, paving the way for European resource and infrastructure integration. But the example of regional cooperation in Europe has proven the exception to the rule. For most of history, the goal of nations has been to conquer land; peace has simply been the time between wars, during which groups prepared for the next conflict.

Modern history has since seen the rise of non-state-centric issues. Socioeconomic gaps between the haves and the have-nots are increasing. This phenomenon is connected to demographics, particularly in Europe—home to approximately fifty million Muslims[7]—and in the United States, where the Hispanic constituency is now an electoral power.[8] Furthermore, ecological issues such as water pollution and greenhouse gases have penetrated international borders, as have issues of human rights—not to speak of the globalized economy.

However, modern history has also seen the number of intense national conflicts and wars grow exponentially. As mentioned in the introduction, the Heidelberg Institute's Conflict Barometer has charted the rise of high- and medium-intensity conflicts, from fewer than twenty in 1945 to one hundred thirty in 2007.[9] An increase in conflicts has resulted in an increase of peace treaties—most of which have floundered.

Reflecting on historical treaties of the past several centuries, it's clear that their purpose has been to consolidate the acquisitions of war and to further traditional aims rather than to aspire to new directions of peaceful relations that emphasize a culture of peace and democratization. These treaties serve to sustain the status quo through the balance of power that results from war, achieving stability via narrow security doctrines based on deterrence. The militant nature of the traditional peace treaty reflects the nature of the peacemaker: most peacemakers are former warmakers who do not rule out the use of force as a possible solution to the conflict. This is true both in the realm of political leadership and in the recruitment of military personnel for peacemaking procedures.

Similarly, peace agreements aimed at consolidating assets, territories, and spheres of influence are not designed to equitably distribute peace dividends. Peace and its dividends have traditionally been claimed by states and their elites and have not been linked to greater social justice or the reduction of socioeconomic gaps. Economics has been represented in traditional peace treaties in terms of spoils emanating from victory, with little mention of economic cooperation between former enemies. The notion of regional development, as well as the role of the international community in strengthening the peace economy, has been largely ignored.

Surprisingly, these gaps are present in peace processes even during this age of globalization. One might have expected globalization to change the nature of peacemaking, to include cooperation within a societal, regional, and global context, emphasizing the values of reconciliation, cooperation, and democratization. On the contrary; although globalization and technology have transformed the world into a global village on one level, particularly in those regions where territory and resources are dominant, peacemaking has not adopted new forms of intercultural exchange and economy.

Simply put, old-fashioned principles of peacemaking are as ineffective in modern times as they were historically, even in places where liberal values of democracy have penetrated legal systems and societies. Peace has not been recognized as a discernible, independent social value. In post-conflict regions, little effort has been made to create a participatory process, to cultivate an environment of peaceful coexistence between former enemies, or to discipline those who are violently opposed to peace.

Modern peace treaties—those of the past fifteen years—continue to fail because they fall into traps of old-fashioned peacemaking. Just like historical peacemaking efforts before them, these modern treaties

1. further traditional aims and dwell on the past;

2. reflect a narrow security doctrine;

3. fail to promote a culture of peace;

4. fail to establish a mechanism against increased socioeconomic gaps;

5. fail to emphasize economic cooperation;

6. lack planning for regional development and international assistance;

7. fail to promote peace socially and politically and lack implied sanctions against domestic opposition; and

8. involve past warmakers acting as peacemakers.

Not every modern peace agreement exhibits all of these flaws —some treaties include progressive peacemaking strategies alongside traditional approaches. Unfortunately, most attempts at modernizing peace have either been buried beneath outdated arrangements or have remained abstract concepts, forgotten by the time implementation rolls around. Here, I explore these core failures of modern peace treaties, using examples of peace agreements from the past decades.

1. **Furthering traditional aims and dwelling on the past.** The Dayton Accords (1995),[10] which were supposed to create peace in the former Yugoslavia, have left much of the region reduced to poverty, with massive economic disruption and persistent instability across the territories where the worst fighting occurred. The accords dealt mostly with the traditional aims of territorial integrity, military aspects of regional stabilization, and boundary demarcation. The wars were the bloodiest conflicts on European soil since the end of World War II, resulting in an estimated 125,000 dead and millions more driven from their homes.[11] Many of the key individual participants were subsequently charged with war crimes. The accords lack clauses relating to reconciliation or strategic peacebuilding efforts.

2. **Reflecting a narrow security doctrine.** The Peace Treaty and Principles of Interrelation between Russian Federation and Chechen Republic Ichkeria (1997) is a perfect example of a narrow security doctrine. The first two clauses of the treaty deal with the rejection of the "use of force" and the development of relationships according to the "norms of international law."[12] Its remaining three clauses have no bearing on peace at all—indeed, hostilities were being

sustained. Similarly, the Khasavyourt Joint Declaration and Principles for Mutual Relations (1996) signed by the Chechen and Russian parties takes into account only the "cessation of military activities" and the "inadmissibility of the use of armed force or threatening its usage."[13]

3. **Failure to promote a culture of peace.** A peace culture was not promoted by the Guatemalan Agreement on a Firm and Lasting Peace (1996).[14] During this civil war, guerilla groups orchestrated coups against the military regimes, an estimated 200,000 people were killed, and many human rights were violated.[15] The agreement outlined a cessation of violence and a redistribution of resources and compensation, but it did not address peacebuilding measures to create a culture of peace. Peace still is not present in Guatemala, more than a decade later.

4. **Failure to establish a mechanism against increased socioeconomic gaps.** More than two million people were displaced and an estimated thirty thousand people were killed during nine years of civil war in which the Sierra Leone government and a rebel group fought over the distribution of that country's resources.[16] The Peace Agreement between the Government of Sierra Leone and the Revolutionary United Front of Sierra Leone (1999)[17] was supposed to end this horrendous civil war; however, the agreement failed to outline methods of decreasing socioeconomic gaps, and to this day the country continues to be wracked with poverty and instability.

5. **Failure to emphasize economic cooperation.** This failure is particularly evident in the peace agreement signed in Khartoum by the government of Sudan and the South Sudan United Democratic Salvation Front (1997).[18] General Omar al-Bashir, head of the Khartoum government, came to power in an Islamist-backed coup in 1989 and had introduced elements of Sharia law, which was opposed by the mainly Christian and animist rebels in the south. The war between northern and southern Sudan has generally been interpreted as a typical ethno-religious conflict between Muslims

and Christians or between Arabs and Africans. Although this characterization was true of the earlier manifestation of the conflict, in the 1950s, and still has some bearing on the recent war, the nature of the conflict has changed. The fighting now is primarily over resources, with the economic and resource crisis in the north emerging as a driving force behind the civil war. The fourth section of the 1997 treaty mentioned a "comprehensive economic and social plan" and the establishment of "development projects," but these were not sufficiently emphasized or developed in this treaty, nor did ensuing agreements and declarations ensure their implementation. Fighting in south Sudan continues to this day.

6. **Lack of planning for regional development and international assistance.** The Belfast Agreement (also known as the Good Friday Agreement) (1998),[19] signed by the British and Irish governments, gained the support of most Northern Ireland political parties, including Sinn Fein (the political wing of the Irish Republican Army), and many of the positive characteristics outlined here are present in that agreement. However, many of the cooperative economic and social projects and other peacebuilding efforts outlined in the agreement have to a large degree not been implemented. Perhaps the addition of a clause relating to international assistance on facilitation and finance would have resulted in more cooperation and more effective implementation of the agreement.

7. **Failure to promote peace socially and politically, and lack of implied sanctions against domestic opposition.** The 1997 treaty between the Russian Federation and Chechen Republic Ichkeria[20] lacks sanctions against domestic opposition. Despite a series of peace agreements (including a cease-fire offered by Chechen President Aslan Mashkadov in June 2000), rebel fighting, suicide attacks, and guerilla warfare by Chechen combatants have continued. Between 300,000 and 600,000 Chechen people are said to have fled their homes as a result of this violence.[21]

8. **Past warmakers acting as peacemakers.** This core failure is manifest in all modern treaties. Of the eight participants who

negotiated the 1999 peace agreement for national reconciliation in Sierra Leone, for example, five were military personnel.[22] Similarly, in Sudan, all parties who negotiated the 1997 peace agreement were military agents.

Sometimes, treaties that end domestic conflict are more realistic than those between countries; they often contain important social rehabilitation, peacebuilding, and developmental elements. The 1996 agreement between Guatemalan rebels and President Alvaro Arzu, and the 1998 Belfast Agreement both hold true to this observation.

In addition to promising an end to a conflict that displaced an estimated one million people,[23] the Guatemalan agreement also outlined land reforms, bilingualism in education, retraining programs for ex-guerrillas, and a decrease in military numbers and budgets. A truth and reconciliation commission headed by a UN official was established in 1994.[24] But implementation failed—as it so often does—and fighting between the military and guerilla groups continues today.

A more successful example is the Belfast Agreement, a major step in the Northern Ireland peace process that began with the 1993 John Hume–Gerry Adams talks. The Belfast Agreement has included peacebuilding activities and some, though not sufficient, economic joint ventures.

On the whole, peacemaking has not experienced a fundamental change since decolonization. In most cases, it still addresses the considerations of the past. With the dissolution of traditional spheres of influence, however, the interests of nation-states have changed. Human nature hasn't changed, but the perception of power has. Power is no longer interpreted as the conquest of land or colonies; the modern world understands power mostly in terms of economics, knowledge, industry, and technology.

Societies may consider war profitable because the victor stands to gain a great deal of power in the modern sense. Nonetheless, truly greater power lies in peace. Peace allows nations to focus their energies on trade, cultural enrichment, and scientific exchange rather than on military expenditures. Peace can be viewed as a tool for change: it does not merely exist in relation to war and the acquisition of territorial assets—it can facilitate stability, cooperation, and mutual enhancement between societies.

To understand peacemaking in an era of globalization and democratization, we need to explore not only modern peace treaties but also decisions and implementation. I have experienced this blessing and burden as Israel's chief negotiator in the Oslo process—a process that made great strides forward but still struggled with the failings of traditional peacemaking, as I will discuss in the next chapter.

CHAPTER TWO

The Oslo Roller Coaster:
A Mixed Model

STARTING IN 1991, CONDITIONS BECAME RIPE FOR PEACE between Israelis and Palestinians. The violent Palestinian uprising known as the First Intifada did not lead to political results for Palestinians and, with the election of an Israeli peace government under Prime Minister Rabin and the first Bush administration's desire to turn the antiwar coalition against Iraq into a pro-peace coalition in the Middle East, the time seemed right to explore options for peace. Negotiations began in Madrid between an Israeli delegation and a Jordanian-Palestinian delegation that included Palestinian representatives of the occupied territories but *not* representatives of the Palestine Liberation Organization (PLO). The talks were later extended to Washington, DC.

But by the end of 1992 those negotiations had stalled. A Norwegian couple, Terje Rod-Larsen (head of a Norwegian NGO dealing with humanitarian conditions in the West Bank and Gaza) and Mona Juul (assistant to Norwegian Foreign Minister Johan Holst), decided to take a different approach. They worked with Israeli Deputy Foreign Minister Yossi Beilin, a staunch peace pioneer, to initiate contact with an official PLO delegation, headed by one of the PLO's senior leaders, Abu Ala. At the beginning of 1993 these talks quickly turned into a secret back-channel negotiation. Whereas the Palestinian representatives took very uncompromising positions during the formal Washington talks, the PLO delegation in Oslo, Norway, was pragmatic and realistic. Yasser Arafat, Yitzhak Rabin, and Shimon Peres were fully in the picture but, although the US administration knew about the back channels, it expressed little hope or interest in them.

By May 1993 the secret channel produced an informal document of principles for an Israeli-Palestinian peace process. It was at this point that the Israeli leadership decided to send an Israeli government official to meet for the first time with the PLO. I was that official.

The first secret PLO-Israeli meeting, between Abu Ala and me, took place on May 21, 1993, in Oslo. Precisely three months later we reached an agreement in principle on a gradual solution to the Palestinian-Israeli conflict—the Declaration of Principles on Interim Self-Government Arrangements (1993). This agreement, also called the Oslo Accord, was recognized by the US administration and was signed in Washington, DC, on September 13, 1993.[1]

The first stage called for an Israeli withdrawal from Gaza and the city of Jericho. The second step called for a gradual Israeli withdrawal from the West Bank cities, coinciding with the first Palestinian presidential and parliamentary elections. These provisions were formalized in the Israeli-Palestinian Interim Agreement on the West Bank and the Gaza Strip, or the Oslo II agreements, signed on September 28, 1995, in Washington.[2] The final stage was to be a three-year negotiation for permanent status and peace between the two sides, resolving all outstanding issues such as borders, refugees, the status of Jerusalem, settlements, and security arrangements. The agreement was coupled with a historic mutual recognition agreement between Israel and the PLO.

The implementation of the agreement proved to be a challenge—much progress on one hand, and setbacks, often turning to violence and terror, on the other. Negotiations between Israel and the PLO continued in the following years, during which our hopes for peace and economic development were juxtaposed with the rapid globalization of the world around us. The process became a roller coaster, and we rode the extremes between euphoria and great disappointment.

February 1994: Davos, Switzerland

In the midst of the Swiss Alps, a tiny, picturesque village became the scene of a most incredible congregation. Inventors, entrepreneurs, heads of multinational institutions, and political leaders came together to design the future at the World Economic Forum. As the heroes and prophets of globalization, these individuals were filled with high hopes for technological revolution, democratization, dissolution of national boundaries, creation of free markets, and free movement of people and goods. Daytime discussions centered on fantastic technological breakthroughs that would translate into social and economic capital, that would establish new dimensions in space and time and would penetrate all physical barriers—achievements to be listed in the scriptures of the world's stock markets.

Such leaps and bounds were reflected in the press, which characterized the "Davos Man" as the new Adam. Indeed, it seemed that participants in the World Economic Forum were creating a new, improved, and sustainable Garden of Eden. The genesis of this era of globalization represented an unwavering faith in the miraculous capacity of the human brain. Humanity's euphoria generated an intense agenda for textbook globalization—industry, competition, information technology, global corporations, biotechnology, high-tech economics, and scientific and economic development—and aimed to bring together the great minds of the new world.

Down the road, another drama was simultaneously unfolding. Deeply covered by a blanket of snow, the Palatin Hotel also was a meeting point of sorts: Israeli Foreign Minister Peres and Palestinian Chairman Arafat had brought their respective negotiating teams to Davos to create the political miracle that ultimately became a mirage. A convergence of historical conflict and dramatic progress, from a tiny land to a new globe, filled us with mesmerizing hope. I took part as Israel's chief negotiator and was firmly dedicated to our strategic goal of removing the bloodstains tainting the relationship between Israelis and Palestinians. We were driven by the desire to join the bullet train of globalization and to work with our former enemies to overcome past conflict.

As the night progressed, the air in the hotel became opaque from anxious cigarette smoking. The World Economic Forum and its globalized ideals became an ironic backdrop; while business and political leaders down the street discussed worldwide open borders, we bickered over the closure of access roads near the Jordan River, which would affect future borders between Israel, Jordan, and the Palestinian Authority. Every meter of land was analyzed in terms of security; the perpetual use of traditional peacemaking methods created the mirage in which we were immersed.

Yet, from the perspective of world leaders, we were inspirational. When Arafat and Peres entered the plenary side by side—two peacemakers, so obviously different in demeanor, apparently ready to contribute positively to their common destiny—three thousand participants burst into a tumultuous standing ovation. At that moment, participants and observers were overwhelmed with the feeling that Israelis and Palestinians could work together to make peace and join the new world order, with globalization as the ultimate prize.

Our euphoria was exploited by the champions of globalization to further strengthen their sense of omnipotence. Davos became synonymous with globalization—but in fact it was homogeneous, ignoring the challenges of a world fractured by old plagues. Not only did the representatives of Africa and other developing regions hardly feature in Davos, but also issues such as hunger, war, disease, and cultural and religious clashes were rarely seriously addressed. Globalization belonged to the profit makers; the rest of the world could take part if and when it reached maturity. Unfortunately, we peacemakers were not yet ripe.

As we met colleagues from other regions, mainly Africa and Europe, who were similarly struggling to bring their nations out of conflict, the Davos event took on new symbolism as an assembly of frustrated peacemakers from around the globe, caught between promise and impotence, attempting to join the new world but unable to make that leap.

October 1994: Casablanca, Morocco

The frustrations and uncertainties of Davos were transformed into hope for the Middle East that October. Under the auspices of King Hassan II of Morocco, hundreds of Israeli businesspeople met in Casablanca with business leaders from Algeria, Egypt, Jordan, Oman, Qatar, Saudi Arabia, Tunisia, and the newly formed Palestinian Authority. Prearranged in late 1993 during a secret meeting between Peres and King Hussein of Jordan,[3] the Casablanca forum aimed to spark economic development and cooperation in the Middle East. It involved Davos Executive Chairman Klaus Schwab; Leslie Gelb, president of the American Council on Foreign Relations; and André Azoulay, the Moroccan peace pioneer and a close advisor to King Hassan II. With the partnership of these individuals and the relentless American peace process coordinator Dennis Ross, I chaired the preparations.

For those short moments in history, the Arab boycott was considered dead. The Promised Land became a land of promise. When the forum met, not a single American, European, or Asian business leader refused an encounter. With our American friends, we planned a regional Middle East bank; other talks centered on innovative programs for public-private partnership. As I looked around the assembly of businesspeople and leaders, I recalled the Davos discussions and allowed myself to hope that a bridge to the new world was within reach.

At the event center, the scorching sun beamed down on us and the sand sprayed in the wind. Entering the royal tent alongside Peres, the heads of state and foreign ministers from at least twelve Arab countries—most wearing traditional jalabyas and kaffiyehs—hovered around our Moroccan host. While we mingled hesitantly, we sensed the genesis of a new era. We discussed the implementation of creative and high-tech projects in an open-border, post-conflict Middle East. One potential project entailed a major tri-national park in the Dead Sea region—an attraction for worldwide tourism. Israelis, Jordanians, and Palestinians had all inherited this historical sea—the lowest point on earth—which, given its environmental uniqueness, could be turned into a major resort area for medical tourism and could become a platform for regional economic development. We believed that our transition from conflict to peace could arouse the interest and energy of the international private sector, could bring life to the Dead Sea. Other proposals included a canal from the Red Sea to the Dead Sea to make our deserts flourish, and industrial parks shared by Israeli and Palestinian entrepreneurs.

Casablanca ended with powerful statements about the future of a new Middle East—but those hopes were short-lived. Ultimately, the Casablanca forum failed to produce even a single project. The necessary bridge between the new world and the old was proving impossible to build. Entrenched in suspicion and animosity, even those mesmerized by the vision of peace had little patience to integrate the interests of nations that, unlike Israel, were not on the high-tech highway. The Middle East, like other transitional regions, remained underdeveloped. The mirage was disappearing.

The private sector decided that regions in transition, such as the Middle East, were a gamble; they did not offer the necessary conditions and incentives for investment. The great promise of public-private partnership was not realized; aid money was earmarked for institution building, security, infrastructure, and, not least, the respective bureaucracies of donors and recipients. Governments were neither psychologically nor practically prepared to provide the foundations necessary to attract investment.

The hopes that germinated in Davos and Casablanca proved transitory. Peace dividends were distributed to an elite minority and not to the wider constituency critical to the success of the process.

Peace became the prize of the wealthy class that was able to jump on the bandwagon of globalization. In response, the majority rebelled against the peace process—at times politically and at times violently. If blame is to be apportioned, much of it belongs to those Israelis and Palestinians who slowed down the process, to the Arab regimes that were not open to economic or political reform, and to the leaders of the international community and globalization, who failed to comprehend that by neglecting the economic challenges of conflict resolution and peacebuilding, they strengthened the forces that would later work to their own detriment.

In contrast to those who promised peace and prosperity, a new coalition began to emerge from the frustration of poverty, the extremism of fundamentalist religious ideologies, and the devastating power of terrorism and weapons of mass destruction. We in the Middle East suspected that, had the Casablanca process been successful, it could have undermined the danger and scope of a potent anti-Western force. But the Davos Men, those champions of New York and Silicon Valley, believed that the path upon which they had embarked should proceed at full pace; patience for their own governments—let alone for latecomers from conflict and post-conflict areas—was limited. Our failure, as members of both the old and new worlds, arose from our lack of progress and our delayed reaction to the imminent and tragic chaos that was approaching.

An Imperfect Peacemaking Parable

Despite the fact that the Oslo process—including the negotiations at Davos and the economic summit at Casablanca—should be viewed retrospectively as a significant and dramatic historical breakthrough toward Middle Eastern peace, the concepts that prodded both sides to their achievements were often outdated. Plenty can be learned from the deficiencies of the Middle East peace. The structural flaws of the Oslo Accords reflect the eight core failures of traditional peace treaties, analyzed in chapter 1.

   1. Oslo **furthered traditional aims and dwelled on the past,**

rather than paving a cooperative road for the future and engaging in a necessary historical reconciliation.

Israelis and Palestinians saw the peace process as a means to advance political and traditional goals and not as a goal in itself. Israel aimed to enhance its security and the Palestinians endeavored to realize their national aspirations. It became evident throughout the process that when reconciliation is not a target in itself even traditional goals will not be achieved.

Peaceful coexistence and cooperative goals can be achieved in a compatible way; this is the true premise of peace. But in the Oslo process the aim of reconciliation and peaceful coexistence was often drowned out by harsh negotiating tactics. Filled with suspicion and constantly competing for the upper hand, the two sides seldom joined hands. Moreover, the rhetoric of our late leaders reflected this antagonism. In May 1994, during a visit to South Africa, Chairman Arafat spoke about the continuation of a holy war—jihad. Prime Minister Rabin responded, "With regard to Arafat's reference to jihad, if in fact he called for jihad … it will place the continuation of the [peace] process between us and the Palestinians in question."[4] Such exchanges were typical of the public rhetoric of these leaders.

The issues negotiated at Oslo included notions of territory, security, the civilian authority of the Palestinian Authority, and mutual recognition between Israel and the PLO. No topic had minor significance; even negotiating the entry point across the Jordan River to the West Bank required three months and two hundred pages of minute agreements. Common interests often became a secondary concern. This myopic attitude undermined the most important strategic issue to be orchestrated—the future relations between Israel and Palestine in the political, economic, and cultural arenas. Such relationships not only would influence the realization of our goals but also would lead to greater regional participation in the process. Sadly, neither side—except perhaps the negotiators themselves—really understood that solutions do not create partnership; rather, partnership creates solutions.

Unfortunately, too, positive intentions between the parties were often overshadowed by larger issues. I recall the initial stages of the permanent-status negotiations that began in May 1996 and took place in Taba, Egypt. During a tête-à-tête after the opening ceremony, Abu Mazen and I concluded that in the first year of negotiations we would focus only on Israeli-Palestinian relations in the year 2000; we would define our strategic aims and tackle only topics relating to our common future. Only then could the strategic goals for 2000 be constructively explored for the permanent-status issues.

But no such negotiations took place. Three weeks after our conversation the Likud came to power in Israel, forming a right-wing coalition. Consequently, sustainable peaceful relations with a Palestinian state were erased as an Israeli aim. At best, the parties were able to micromanage the process until its near-death.

2. Oslo **reflected a narrow security doctrine** based on deterrence and an irrelevant balance of power, rather than creating the motivation to sustain peace.

In line with the centuries-old security doctrine, the primary consideration during negotiations at Oslo was to deter the enemy from developing military capacity and thereby threatening the peace. The Israeli team made it clear from the outset of the Oslo process that Israel would maintain overall responsibility for security. Despite any civilian or military authority transferred to the Palestinian Authority, Israel would retain the right to physically intervene if a security threat developed.

In May 1994 apprehension stirred regarding the potential contradiction between a security-based agreement and an economically based agreement. Israel and the PLO had concluded an agreement in Cairo, Egypt, that outlined Israel's military withdrawal from most of Gaza and Jericho. The Cairo Agreement implied very stringent security arrangements to prevent terror.[5] At the same time, they had also signed the Paris Economic Agreement, which would facilitate the development of the Palestinian economy and the freedom of movement of goods and people.[6] But such freedom of movement presented a potential security concern, provoking Israel to insist that in the case of a contradiction between the two accords, the Cairo Agreement would take precedence—another victory for the dominance of security.

The security doctrine derives from an era when employing military tactics was assumed to achieve deterrence. Today, with the accelerated development of ballistic weapons and the proliferation of terrorism fueled by deprivation and poverty, such a doctrine is no longer appropriate. In simple terms, economy not only outweighs security, it actually provides security. The growth of the Palestinian economy should have been a clear Israeli security interest, but it was not treated as such.

3. Oslo **failed to promote a culture of peace** by introducing the necessary values and beliefs.

War creates a culture of hostility, victimization, and suspicion. Only this kind of culture can provide the impetus for people to sacrifice their lives and the lives of their children. Changing this culture of war to a culture of peace must be the desire of those involved in the peace process. And although such hopes are often expressed in songs and poetry, the transformation is difficult to achieve.

During the Oslo period, there were days permeated by a sense of cultural transformation; dramatic media events often sparked feelings of euphoria. But reality fell short of expectations. The provocative rhetoric of leaders perpetuated stereotypes of the "other side" and sustained the culture of hostility. Israelis and Palestinians remained foreign to one another (except on the battleground), and person-to-person encounters of any significance were almost nonexistent.

The mass media, too, avoided creating a culture of peace. In times of conflict, the media were virtually recruited to the struggle; during the peace process, the mutual demonization in the media continued, even during days of relative quiet, catering to existing preconceptions in public opinion, which had been molded during the days of terror and military activity.

4. Oslo **failed to establish a mechanism against increased socio-economic gaps,** which turned the peace process into a revolution of the wealthy rather than a means of dispensing peace dividends more equally.

One measure of peace is wealth. When conflict decreases, so docs the risk of doing business, and new investment opportunities arise. However, in the case of Israel and the Palestinian Authority, only a small elite on both sides of the Green Line (the 1949 cease-fire line) reaped any peace dividends. In Israel, the champions of the high-tech industry acquired the capital, while in the Palestinian Authority, the higher echelons of the PLO leadership, which had arrived in the West Bank and Gaza from Tunis, enjoyed increased influence. At best, the middle and lower classes in both societies maintained their standards of living.

As a result of peace, the socioeconomic gap in each society grew. Palestinians in refugee camps saw their brethren make homes for themselves in Gaza-style skyscrapers. Israelis struggling to feed their children in south Tel Aviv watched their fellow citizens in the north of the city board private jets. The poorer echelons in both societies generally saw peace as a betrayal, and they rebelled—some politically, others violently. It is exactly this economic gap that endangers political stability.

5. Oslo **failed to emphasize economic cooperation,** to create common interests and greater interdependence.

Despite the agreements and their partial implementation, the economic reality on the ground remained essentially unchanged from the days of full occupation: two islands standing side by side—a strong Israel and a weak, dependent Palestinian Authority. Few people paid attention to the two economic annexes of the 1993 Oslo Declaration of Principles, which addressed the concept and benefits of economic integration. One annex discussed the Palestinian economy and Israeli-Palestinian economic cooperation; the other emphasized a regional economic plan for the Middle East.

Unfortunately, the implementation process did not furnish the economic cooperation that would have narrowed the enormous gap between the Israeli and Palestinian economies. Israel contributed the minimum allocation in customs and taxes that was due to the Palestinian Authority for Palestinian goods, and the Palestinians were more committed to the flag and to independence than to taking advantage of financial mechanisms on offer for their development and prosperity.

Moreover, the idea of enhancing the Palestinian economy as part of peacebuilding projects was almost totally overlooked. There were some modest exceptions—the creation of one or two industrial parks, limited cooperation in the field of information technology, and a joint technology fund—but these advancements melted away in the wake of violence and terror. There also was little cooperation in construction; not even one project involved professionals from both sides. Ultimately, the export of goods and services within Palestinian areas declined by 5.4 percent between 1993 and 2003.[7]

6. Oslo **lacked planning for regional development and international assistance**; international aid was geared toward traditional bilateral programs and bureaucracies rather than toward supporting a cooperative economic peace.

Although much of the negotiation that took place in the Oslo process was bilateral, the international community played an important role in encouraging the process and created massive aid packages for the benefit of the regimes. However, traditional peace aid policies had little effect on peace itself because the international community, led by the United States and the European Union, differentiated between aid for development and aid for peacebuilding.

This separation of aid funding proved detrimental. Israel and the Palestinian Authority, combined, received about $10 billion of special aid throughout the Oslo process. Israel received from the United States aid for security measures, and the Palestinians received civilian aid, among the highest per capita in the world. Bilateral aid mechanisms were searching for local flagship projects that had high aid-bureaucracy overhead. The multilateral mechanisms of the World Bank and the United Nations viewed aid linked to peace projects as almost taboo. Instead, the aid would go to Palestine as a developing country, as if peace was not the issue. Funds actually earmarked for Palestinian-Israeli cooperation did not target the sort of public diplomacy and peacebuilding that would have affected public opinion.

I was present during the US Agency for International Development's talks regarding agricultural projects in the Palestinian Authority. We suggested an initiative that would allow Israeli farmers to work with Palestinian farmers rather than with agrarian experts from Arizona who knew very little about the region's soil. Israeli and Palestinian experts working together on similar land, with similar interests, could have inspired a peacebuilding trend and a sustainable project between neighbors. But our suggestion was in vain. Because the international community insisted upon separating development and peace, the lack of funding was harmful on both ends.

7. Oslo **failed to promote peace socially and politically and lacked implied sanctions against domestic opposition.**

An important element of peacemaking is the shaping of a national identity. There was violent opposition to the Oslo process from both camps, with each side espousing messianic views of saving their respective countries from evil by projecting patriotism and nationalism. These detractors warned against open society, westernization, and liberalism. Peace can never be achieved without the defeat of such opposition or by the politics of consensus. But the choir of religious nationalism became the backdrop to the assassination of Prime Minister Rabin, and the Palestinian chairman's power weakened in proportion to his inability and unwillingness to challenge his violent opposition. That decisive internal battle never took place, as both sides essentially tried to appease the enemy from within.

A unique challenge for Israel surfaced in February 1994 when Jewish fanatic Baruch Goldstein murdered twenty-nine Palestinian worshippers in Hebron.[8] The Palestinian demand to evacuate four hundred Jewish settlers from the old city of Hebron was understandable; the city's 150,000 Palestinians were living in a state of perpetual violence, which curtailed the settlers' freedom of movement.[9] It seemed that at that moment of shock, most Israelis would have condoned such a move.

Along with several colleagues from the Israel Defense Forces, I boarded a plane to Tunis to meet Arafat, who persisted with the question of the Hebron settlers. We knew from Rabin and Peres that about half the settlers would be evacuated. Yet, after the plane landed in Tunis, we were informed that the settler evacuation plan had been canceled due to the potential for violence on the part of other settlers, following the evacuation. Apparently, Chief of Staff Ehud Barak had convinced Rabin to postpone the necessary confrontation indefinitely.

Similar trepidation existed on the Palestinian side. Prior to the Israeli elections of the fourteenth Knesset in February 1996, I met Arafat in Gaza to request that he take all necessary measures to prevent terrorism during the Israeli election campaign, as we had credible intelligence that Iranian elements were masterminding terror attacks to advance a right-wing election victory that would sabotage the peace process. An empty promise on Arafat's part resulted in four suicide bombs exploding in Jerusalem and Tel Aviv during February and March. Exactly as we had warned, these bombings had the calculated devastating impact on the Israeli psyche and brought about a right-wing election victory.

To move toward peace and quash archaic antipeace forces, an element of civil war and cultural confrontation is necessary, to bolster the very nature and identity of the peacemaking society. Tragically, the domestic policy of the two governments during the Oslo process simply safeguarded the politics of seeking the broadest consensus possible.

8. Oslo **involved warmakers acting as peacemakers,** and too many of these former warriors believed that certain situations could only be resolved by force.

The pioneers of the peace process were peace-obsessed, and the decision makers, including Rabin, Peres, and—at least initially—Arafat, were extremely courageous to take the unpopular route of compromise. Nonetheless, the bulk of the peacemakers at Oslo were former warmakers. The Israeli side comprised army generals and heads of the secret service, while the Palestinian side was made up of leaders of the First Intifada and terror activists. The argument that army personnel make good peacemakers because they have seen the price of war couldn't be further from the truth. Although there are some exceptional cases (for example, Lieutenant General Lipkin-Shahak, a former Israel Defense Forces chief of staff), most people who have seen the use of power as a solution continue to do so and, worse, continue to use it. Professional warmakers will almost always maintain a safety net to be employed in a worst-case scenario; deterrence will always be preferred over building trust. During the Oslo process, this mind-set became self-fulfilling. Those of us with a civilian mind-set of peaceful coexistence as the only option were in the minority.

The Oslo process was undoubtedly a historic breakthrough; without these peace accords, the West Bank and Gaza might have been annexed to Israel, resulting in total turmoil, anarchy, and a binational state. Oslo took courage and ingenuity, but the process—not unlike other global peace processes—had structural flaws, mostly related to the fact that both parties consistently exploited the past while supposedly working for the future. Being from the Middle East, we would always be confused by our dichotomized identity, which is based in both modernity and antiquity. Although the process was politically and morally legitimate and pointed in the right direction, the implementation of the Oslo process was overburdened by the inertia of the past.

In February 1997 a group of frustrated peace professionals congregated at the sidelines of another globalization conference in Davos. Representatives from the Middle East, former Yugoslavia,

Ireland, and South Africa gathered for another four days of meetings. The Davos crowd hailed our appearance but did not absorb us into their world. We were encouraged to abandon our conflicts, but in one way or another all of us repeated, at least partially, old-fashioned slogans that focused on resolving past issues rather than future ones and on supporting outdated security doctrines. We were overwhelmed by a culture of confrontation, unable to embrace the new economy of integration. Every issue—economy, education, conviction, health, and nutrition—was being "modernized" with a view to the future. Every issue except the one that ruled them all: peace.

PART II

A New Model

The Four Pillars of Modern Peace

A New Model

IMAGINE COUNTRIES A AND B MAKING EFFORTS TO MOVE beyond bitter conflicts and toward a peaceful coexistence. The atmosphere at the negotiating table is stiff with hatred and suspicion; thousands of citizens on both sides of the border have fled, been killed, or been deported during the conflict. Only a slim majority of either society yearns for a compromising peace. But delegates, endeavoring to demonstrate such compromise, meticulously negotiate a new border.

Negotiations emphasize traditional peacemaking parameters relating to the deployment of armies away from the border, the monitoring of troop deployment, and the stationing of UN peacekeeping forces along the border. The countries establish diplomatic and commercial relations and facilitate visitation rights for their respective citizens. The international community provides aid to both countries, simultaneously applauding the success of the agreement. Rumors drift around the globe that the leaders of the two countries are likely candidates for the Nobel Peace Prize.

The above scenario paints a promising and familiar picture. Let us continue on this hypothetical path with the following realistic developments occurring in both countries:

- Opposition groups protest "peace," threatening the use of violence both domestically and internationally.

- Mainstream media outlets are skeptical of the "enemy's" motivation and present public opinion polls that illustrate growing opposition toward the agreements.

45

- Militaries accuse one another of border troop deployment beyond the quotas allowed by the agreement.

- Scandals involving corruption and the misuse of aid money are reported, weakening the support of the disillusioned constituency.

- Opposition parties accuse the political leadership of defeatism and corruption.

- Terror attacks are launched by members of country B against civilians in country A, arousing military retaliation and halting economic cooperation.

- The UN Security Council convenes to attempt to enforce the original agreement.

- Terrorism continues and country A occupies territory whence terror is launched.

- Attacks and counterattacks become daily events.

- End of peace.

Such a scenario is not farfetched; indeed, it features actual events from several international situations. Years are spent negotiating hundreds of pages of agreements, outlining new borders and intended diplomatic and commercial relations. More time is squandered in deliberating troop deployment, and intelligence technology is installed for its monitoring. Such agreements present a combination of legal jargon and technical, security, and diplomatic arrangements. Yet, even with all the meticulous work that negotiations of this nature entail, neither peace nor stability can be ensured. Peace applies to two societies, not simply to two armies and two foreign ministries.

Our theoretical scenario can be transformed into a different picture by adding elements after the peace agreement is signed:

- The building of roads and railways between country A and B is planned and implemented, creating jobs in the short term and interconnectivity in the long term. Jobs are channeled to more needy populations.

- Both countries work to establish tourism infrastructure within the border region and introduce a parallel marketing campaign to attract tourists to special cross-border attractions.

- A sister-city program is implemented to link municipalities, businesses, civil society organizations, and youth exchange programs.

- Both countries establish cross-border qualified industrial zones for joint businesses, enhancing joint export to Europe, the United States, and Asia.

- Joint media, films, and documentaries are released to generate a more positive peace culture.

- A joint public relations campaign is implemented to strengthen the voice of the latent and silent peaceful majority.

- A vast program of security cooperation is implemented, including joint forces against terrorism.

With these cooperative elements in place, peace has a better chance of being stable and sustainable. However, to move effectively from security-centric concepts to joint social, economic, and cultural components, we must systematically analyze the main areas of participatory peace and decide how to treat them during negotiations, agreements, and implementation. In other words, we need a new peacemaking model that treats these issues as central to the process instead of peripheral.

This book presents just such a model, starting with the four pillars that must be central to every peace process:

1. **Participatory peace and glocalization.** A process of decentralization based on building a bridge between global opportunities and local players, particularly through city-to-city interactions and youth empowerment.

2. **Peace ecology.** The movement from a culture of war to a culture of peace based on common values, tolerance, and coexistence.

3. **Peacebuilding.** The creation of joint cross-border ventures in the political, economic, cultural, and social spheres.

4. **Creative diplomacy.** The use of innovative approaches to past problems, focusing on what both sides stand to gain rather than on what concessions each side will have to make.

These pillars are discussed in detail in the following chapters, along with practical guidance for implementation and real-life case studies that integrate these concepts into peacemaking initiatives.

CHAPTER THREE

Participatory Peace
and Glocalization

GLOBALIZATION WAS CELEBRATED AS THE PEACE OF OUR generation. It promised a world without borders, a global village in which communication, travel, trade, and consumption would be universal. By wearing jeans, eating at McDonald's, and watching MTV, the people of the world could reconcile under the umbrella of a single megaculture and advance a common experience of peace and prosperity.

True, globalization has produced important achievements in the developed world as well as in Asia, Latin America, and Eastern Europe, but it has not created the anticipated paradise. The blanket of globalization simply did not cover everyone. Much of the world's population remains deeply entrenched in poverty, disease, and violence; these populations struggle beyond the walls of the revolution. Moreover, in many cases these societies not only were deprived of the benefits of globalization but also fell victim to it. Globalization had, at least in their eyes, usurped their identities and attempted to impose upon them a cultural, political, and economic system that was at odds with their traditions, values, and capacities.

Awareness of this dark underbelly of globalization was limited, particularly with respect to Africa. During those days in Casablanca when we dreamed of joining the rest of the world as party to the Davos globalization, neither the political nor the economic leadership was moved by the genocide that took place a few thousand miles south, in Rwanda, where 850,000 people were killed within three months.[1] A world of globalization euphoria existed alongside a world of vast suffering; an invisible wall divided them.

Those who grow up in the globalized world enjoy the most advanced health services and technology and the opportunity to realize one's full intellectual potential. In such societies, war has by and large become a historical narrative. On the developed side of the invisible wall, one's chance of survival past the age of five is greater than 99 percent. In Sierra Leone, however, approximately every fourth child dies before the age of five,[2] plagued by malaria, AIDS, diarrhea, or other health problems primarily affecting developing countries. The children who endure these health threats are often recruited to become child soldiers.[3]

The globalized and unglobalized worlds are extremely foreign to each another. Consider the following:

- An estimated 2.6 billion people (nearly half the world's population) live on a per capita income of under $2 per day[4]—less than what the average European cow receives in subsidies.[5]

- In Sierra Leone, less than $40 per year per person is spent on health, compared to more than $6,000 per person in the United States.[6]

- Under-five mortality is fifteen times higher in low-income countries than in high-income countries.[7]

- Most developing countries currently suffer, or have suffered in recent years, from conflict.

- Conflict is estimated to have caused more than 300,000 deaths in the year 2000 alone, with more than half of these deaths occurring in Africa. Direct mortality from conflict accounts for 0.5 percent of all mortality.[8]

- Twenty percent of the world's population enjoys 80 percent of the world's resources.[9]

Although some developing countries are trying to meet the globalization criteria and enter the Emerald City, others are expressing frustration and hatred through violence. Such countries provide fertile ground for fundamentalists and extremist anti-Westerners.

Afghanistan is a prime example. On September 11, 2001, the invisible wall collided with the twin towers of the World Trade Center in New York. Al-Qaida itself did not act out of poverty and misery, but its base of support lies among the have-nots and those estranged from Western culture.

Following the tragic events of September 11, Americans were left wondering in genuine astonishment, "Why do they hate us?" The answer is dichotomous: although most developing countries would prefer to be American allies, there also exists deep antagonism toward the superpower and its allies. According to a post–September 11 Pew Global Attitudes survey, the United States remains substantially mistrusted by the rest of the world.[10] September 11 was a rude awakening that united the Western world; it was an attack against the symbol of US and Western power. The result was not only a collaborative focus on terrorism but also a clearer understanding that much of the world has not realized the prosperity of globalization.

The United States and its allies went to war to punish those responsible and the countries that supported them, but success is still distant in Afghanistan and Iraq. It has become clear to both the United States and Europe that technological, military, and economic power does not protect them against people hidden in caves. US trade can reach Kabul in no time, but weapons—including potential weapons of mass destruction—can depart Kabul just as easily. The "local" arena has become fertile turf from which fanatics can attack global power. Globalization has boomeranged.

This is not the forum in which to fully analyze the nature of globalization or its place in today's world. We must, however, weigh its repercussions on our generation's peace and diplomacy. It has become clear that the world needs a bridge between the global and the local.

The bridges that exist have had limited success. Although Western military deterrence has influenced the regimes in Afghanistan and Iraq, it has not succeeded in pushing other regions into a pro-Western, antiterror camp, as is exemplified by Iran, Syria, and Gaza.

And although in absolute terms economic aid and debt forgiveness seem substantial, their effects are limited by the bureaucracies of the donors and recipients, and, in some cases, by the corruption of the latter. The gap between the haves and have-nots remains colossal, maintaining the potential for international turmoil.

Democratization is the cornerstone of the US administration, and if the world followed the gospel of Thomas Jefferson, perhaps peace would reign. However, even countries that yearn for freedom fight its imposition by the United States. Democratization is a long and arduous process and must germinate and evolve from a country's roots if it is to embody the individual culture of each country.

Present bridges focus on relationships between governments, but to facilitate cultural understanding and peaceful coexistence we must link the global and the local—hence, "glocalization."

The Power of the City

The channel for glocalization must be a political entity with clout. The one sociopolitical unit that is gaining power in the era of globalization, while also remaining closest to the needs and aspirations of citizens, is the city.

In 1930, seven hundred million people, representing 30 percent of the world's population, lived in urban areas.[11] Today, that number has increased dramatically; 2007 was the first year in which more people were living in urban areas than in rural areas.[12] Cities have become our primary social unit, and in both the developed and the developing worlds cities are eagerly stepping into the voids created by the decline of national boundaries and the erosion of the power of the nation-state.

Cities can reach people in ways that nations cannot. Cities have the flexibility to adapt large-scale programs to local needs and resources. They can plan modern, urban infrastructure to deal with the massive influx of people joining city peripheries, particularly in the developing world. Cities can push for tourism on a level that is impossible for national governments, creating tailored marketing plans for local sites and museums.

Where youth is concerned, cities have the ability to bring the younger generation together on a local scale. Cities can work closely with children to provide basic necessities, can create a youth-empowerment agenda for the future, and can encourage interactions among youth from different cities.

Cities also have greater control over their relationship to other cities in the areas of media, art, sports, economics, and trade. The forging of city-to-city relationships through economic and social activity and exchange can help connect the local and global. In 2001, one of the organizations over which I preside—the Glocal Forum in Rome—initiated city projects related to diplomacy. The aim of the Glocal Forum is to create a balance between the global and the local—to glocalize peace and development through city-to-city interactions. With projects in over one hundred forty cities worldwide and relationships with nearly one hundred partners from the public and private sectors, the Glocal Forum is making great strides toward decentralizing the peace process and inviting the participation of more people from all levels of society.

One event initiated by the Glocal Forum is the annual Glocalization Conference, which began in 2002. These conferences bring city representatives together in an effort to engender city-to-city relationships across borders and conflict zones. For example, at the second annual Glocalization Conference, in Rome, a roundtable discussion took place between mayors of the conflict cities Addis Ababa (Ethiopia) and Asmara (Eritrea), Belgrade (Serbia) and Priština (Kosovo), Nablus (Palestinian Authority) and Rishon Le-Zion (Israel), and Delhi (India) and Karachi (Pakistan). James Wolfensohn—one of the most prominent statesmen and economists in the world and president of the World Bank at that time—was present, and the conference moderator was Terje Rod-Larsen, who is a peacemaker to the core. Neither, however, was required to use his diplomatic skills—a common language among the mayors was already manifest. They were ready to engage with one another for peaceful coexistence and for the good of their cities' citizens.

The intention of the conference was to facilitate links between two cities representing states in conflict. These links required cooperation based on the empowerment of local governments in project implementation, youth empowerment for the same purpose, and a connection between the development-based economic aspects and the peacebuilding aspects of the project. Although these links required political support, they also demanded less bureaucracy and more social participation.

The encounter between the mayors of Delhi and Karachi was typical. By coincidence, they entered the arrival hall of the Rome airport at the same moment, and only one driver was present to pick them up. It was then that they discovered the "unpleasant" surprise of their mutual presence. The traffic jams of Rome afforded them time to break the ice, and by the time they reached the hotel the concept of a youth exchange (ultimately facilitated by the World Bank) was set in stone. That program is still running.

Mayors as the New Peace Leaders

The connection between the mayors of Delhi and Karachi is exactly the sort of relationship that should be appreciated and encouraged in modern peacemaking. With the erosion of national governments' powers as a result of globalization, the powers and responsibilities of cities and local governments have increased. Today, mayors are catering to most of their citizens' needs, including low-income housing, street infrastructure, social services, education, health, and the public order. Citizens are becoming locally patriotic and are getting increasingly involved in their cities. The city provides a meeting point between global and local forces. It attracts the benefits of globalization but remains local; it uses Microsoft Windows while peering through the backyard window.

Mayors and local governments are thus well positioned to lead peacebuilding efforts. Less hindered by bureaucracies and political dogmas than their national counterparts, mayors share a common urban dialogue that allows them to communicate and cooperate on a pragmatic basis. Close to the people, they can mobilize their civil societies to take an active part in the consolidation and preservation of peace through economic and social cooperation across the conflict divide. Local actors not only should be the beneficiaries of peace initiatives but also should be empowered as vital agents to demonstrate the benefits of coexistence in the day-to-day experience of post-conflict communities. City-to-city cooperation can facilitate a participatory process and create a constituency for peace; misguided stereotypes can be shattered and peace dividends can extend beyond elite groups to benefit broad sectors of society.

Mayors sometimes need a little encouragement to connect with their cross-border counterparts. In September 2002 I found myself waiting at the Athens municipality with Ghassan Shaka'a, a senior leader of the PLO and mayor of the city of Nablus, the most populated city in the West Bank, and my friend Meir Nitzan, mayor of Rishon Le-Zion, one of Israel's wealthiest and largest cities. We were to meet with Dimitris Avramopoulos, the mayor of Athens and a staunch proponent of cities' engagement in diplomatic efforts. The wait was uncomfortable, to say the least.

"Nothing will come out of this. All common ground is lost," Nitzan whispered to me, while Shaka'a's demeanor exposed his desperation to abandon ship.

Forty-five minutes later, the two mayors departed the meeting having forged a close friendship that continues to this day. During the meeting, they spoke about their responsibilities to their citizens and youth and discussed day-to-day management of sewage problems and transportation planning. Both men had profound disdain for their respective national governments, believing that the national leaders had virtually abdicated their responsibilities to their people's real needs. A union of sorts was born, surprising both Israelis and Palestinians.

This union launched a broader initiative for making pragmatic and down-to-earth contacts between Israeli and Palestinian mayors. A few months later, the Israeli mayors of Rishon Le-Zion, Ra'anana, and Ashdod, together with Palestinian mayors from Nablus and Qalqilya, were hosted by the mayor of Rome, Walter Veltroni. Within forty-eight hours we had created the Rome Understanding, a document dealing with a long-term vision of peace, according to which "the two states, Israel and Palestine, will live side by side in peace, security, and mutual dignity." The understanding included a program of "socioeconomic as well as people-to-people cooperation on the local level" and agreeably addressed issues of permanent status.

The text was embraced by both the Israeli and the Palestinian unions of local government, and Nablus and Rishon Le-Zion immediately began to cooperate. Youth from both cities now engage in an Internet-based pen pal project and have developed a municipal youth community to deal with youth-related issues and cooperative practices. Additionally, youth from Rishon Le-Zion assisted youth from Nablus in establishing a municipal youth council to meet the needs of the youth in the city.

With the impetus of Israel's disengagement from Gaza, and in the aftermath of the 2007 Annapolis Conference, the Rome Understanding can be applied to additional cities within Israel by twinning them with Palestinian cities. A network of municipal youth councils, established across Israel and Palestine and facilitated by the international community, not only will help young people resist the temptations of Hamas and other terrorist organizations but also will foster the creation of a platform for close cooperation on a grassroots level—a more effective method than any anti-terrorist strategy.

Since the summer of 2001, I have been meeting with mayors from around the globe and facilitating their interconnectivity. I have discovered that local governments generally possess a down-to-earth attitude, a pragmatic managerial capacity, and a better understanding of people's needs than their national counterparts.

All of these characteristics are vital to peacemaking and peace-building. Mayors and their staffs can serve as modern-day diplomats; through decentralization—or glocalization—cities bring practical and powerful capacities to the peace table. City diplomacy must be undertaken by local players so that they can act on the global map of peacebuilding and development.

A Direct Line to Citizens

Because mayors are so much closer to their citizens than national governments, they can cut out the excesses of national bureaucracy and the irrelevant elements in peacebuilding projects. The Rome-Kigali connection, facilitated by the Glocal Forum, illustrates how city-to-city interactions can be both more efficient and more effective than large-scale aid programs implemented on a national level.

I met Theoneste Mutsindashyaka—the young, charismatic mayor of the Rwandan capital of Kigali—during the first Glocalization Conference in Rome, in May 2001. In his soft voice, he recalled the horrific saga of the Rwandan genocide and the deep wounds that penetrated his city. With the support of the Glocal Forum, we decided to create the first concrete North-South intercity developmental project, a partnership between the cities of Rome and Kigali, to contribute to the internal peace of Rwanda.

The project was spearheaded by an urban agricultural project on Kigali's periphery. The Italian government transferred most of the funds to execute the project through the city of Rome, which itself invested 15 percent of the budget. The UN's Food and Agriculture Organization worked with the municipality of Kigali to plan and develop the project, which included the establishment of local associations on rehabilitated wetlands and in hill areas, the development of microgardens, and the creation of animal-breeding and forestry associations. Agricultural experts from the Roman municipality worked with their counterparts in Kigali, with both sides contributing equal knowledge. (In city-to-city cooperation, the North must admit what it needs to learn, rather than lecturing the South or imposing what it thinks the South needs. Capacity building goes both ways.)

The project brought former enemies together in a constructive way. Hutus and Tutsis, the genocide survivors, worked side by side, as did soldiers who had returned from the Congolese border. A study by the Italian research company CERFE, commissioned by the World Bank, illustrated the project's cost-effectiveness: the cost of overhead was 6.5 percent—much more efficient than state-to-state projects, which have administrative overhead of up to 30 or 40 percent.[13] This difference is due to the fact that national governments hire more—and more expensive—consultants. As a result, the quantities and benefits of aid that actually reach the needy are far greater in intercity aid projects than in interstate aid projects. In this project, a model was created for future peacebuilding projects channeled through cities.

More importantly, the project inspired Rome-Kigali municipal staff and civil society relations in all directions. In Kigali, the mayor of Rome hosted a roundtable discussion between interested individuals and groups, replacing costly consultants and bureaucracies with civil society. A Rome delegation of ten people visited Kigali to learn its needs. Shortly thereafter, the municipality of Rome supplied toys and recreational units for children, provided important medication to Kigali hospitals, and helped facilitate, through Rome Sports University, a marathon and a sports training unit in Kigali. The energy of social goodwill met the needs and enthusiasm of a society in Kigali struggling to come to peace with itself. The Rome-Kigali connection brought more people into the peace process and cut out the waste and anonymity of national programs.

Another example that proves the great potential of city-to-city developments is the astounding success of the Glocal Forum's We Are the Future program, initiated by Quincy Jones (a music legend and man of peace), my good Palestinian friend Hani Masri, and me. Jones penetrated the mind-set of people throughout the world, raising both awareness and funding to tackle the poverty, hunger, and conflict in Africa, with his 1985 aid venture represented by the famous song "We Are the World." However, his projects were not sustainable, and much of the money evaporated into the hands of corrupt African governments.

Jones was disappointed, but he refused to give up. He became drawn to the concept of working with local governments and, together with Hani Masri, we initiated the We Are the Future program for children who were victims of war in seven conflict cities: Addis Ababa; Asmara; Kabul; Kigali; Nablus; Freetown, Sierra Leone; and to some degree Rishon Le-Zion, as a partner of Nablus. The beneficiaries received goods, services, and a holistic approach to education in the areas of nutrition, medicine, sports, and computers.

The project was ignited by a massive concert in Rome in 2004 that featured a mosaic of pop, reggae, Asian, Arabic, and Hebrew songs performed for a half million captivated spectators. Stars included Santana, Nora Jones, Oprah Winfrey, and Angelina Jolie as well as local performers from Iraq, the Palestinian Authority, Rwanda, and Israel.[14] The exposure resulted in close to forty developed cities volunteering to become peer cities to the seven conflict cities.

One such relationship was created between the North American city of Baltimore, Maryland, and Freetown, one of the world's poorest cities. During meetings between the two mayors it was revealed that the biggest killer after the war was malaria, which often resulted from a lack of proper sanitation. Only two garbage trucks were available to take care of the sanitary disaster that had engulfed Sierra Leone's capital city. Within days, Baltimore arranged for two more garbage trucks to be deployed in Freetown. US companies and organizations partnered with the municipality to provide the aid that Freetown required. In this case—as in so many others—it was the *city* that was able to communicate its particular needs on a global level. Glocalization had affected development and peace.

Iraq's process of democratization and development might have looked different if its rehabilitation had reflected the way it was conquered—city by city. The concept of glocalization could facilitate links for development capacity and peacebuilding among Baghdad, Basra, and Mosul and US and British cities.

Most people covet peace but lack faith in the other side's ability to nurture it. Glocalization can recruit societies to be part of the peace process and channel their existing goodwill into cooperation; its essential power lies in the link between local government and civil society, which continues to grow with time. The democratization of peace is not about the imposition of democracy on nondemocratic regimes but about the participation of societies in peace processes, where they often encounter the former enemy on a cooperative basis for the first time. A worldwide, participatory social network led by local governments can be created, generating a better balance between the beaming powers of globalization and those left in the shadow of conflict and misery.

CHAPTER FOUR

Peace Ecology

SOCIETIES THAT HAVE ENDURED CONFLICT FOR GENERATIONS
are understandably highly suspicious of their former enemies; this
suspicion comes out in hostility and aggression. The compromises
and cooperation that are so necessary to the peace process are
often perceived as betrayals. Leaders and negotiators treat their
peace partners as enemies and are overcautious of working together
toward reconciliation. People even feel comfortable with the status
quo of suspicion, because there is always someone else to blame
for one's predicament.

For real peace to thrive, a fundamental change in the peacemaking environment must occur. This transformation can be derived
from those inside the conflict area and from those beyond the regional boundaries. An integrative strategy can be planned and implemented to ensure that peace is not created in a vacuum; parallel to
conflict resolution, both sides must move from a culture of war to a
culture of peace—in other words, societies must create and nourish
a peace ecology.

Outside influence is of great strategic importance; by infiltrating
the conflict region during the process of resolution, the international community can demonstrate its support of the post-conflict societies. Although conflict societies may feel a dangerous comfort in
insularity, there is a simultaneous, contrary desire to be released from
a fortress mentality—the populations should be open and should
allow peaceful and cooperative values to penetrate. Peacemaking
itself is not a detached value; it can be supplemented by important
humanitarian values that influence the identities of post-conflict

countries and develop a regional identity as part of the reconciliation process.

In any bilateral negotiation, regional partners can convene and declare a long-term vision of the region, based on common values of peace, humaneness, and cooperation. By definition, conflicts create ghettos with almost impenetrable walls. Countries in conflict reflect each other's suspicion and antagonism. During Israeli-Palestinian negotiations, for example, our common language of victimization surfaced; looking at the enemy was like looking in the mirror.

Common Values Are Key

The key to creating a peace ecology lies in the value system that can be introduced into the core conflict area. Paradoxically, it is easier to define a common vision among many players than between two negotiating partners terrified of concessions. An atmosphere of peace can help coax negotiators toward common goals. The process must not be bogged down by details that lead to negative interpretations of the process by disillusioned constituencies.

The core conflict area can be greatly influenced by positive values common to the greater region. The process can be further stimulated by regional cooperation in areas such as water sharing, dealing with refugees, economic development, and environmental conservation. Such social development can help the peacemaking effort by facilitating the necessary free movement of goods, people, and—no less important—ideas. To create a peace ecology, regional cooperation can take both tangible and psychological forms.

A peace ecology can reframe compromises as advancements rather than concessions; in this light, negotiations have the potential to become a win-win situation instead of a hierarchical or competitive debate. Most importantly, a peace ecology places coexistence on the basis of equality as a core value that eventually becomes organic within a society.

The development of a peace ecology is fraught with obstacles, but it is essential. To begin, the cancerous atmosphere of conflict and war must be uprooted. In conflict situations the enemy is dehumanized, equal rights are relinquished, and it is difficult to let go of the perception of the former enemy as the culprit. In a conflict narrative each side tries to monopolize suffering, defending its own virtue and portraying the Other as the aggressor. Often, all sides approach the negotiating table with the attitude that they—and they alone—deserve justice, security, and retribution.

In a peace ecology narrative, all sides *do* deserve these things. Modern negotiations must stem from fair, mutual perceptions of the Other and must acknowledge that both sides equally seek and deserve justice, security, and prosperity. As long as either side dehumanizes the other or maintains perceptions of inequality, the conflict will never be resolved.

The Role of the Media

The media exerts massive influence on societies' perceptions and values. Media coverage of events can make or break positive public opinion about peace and cannot be fully orchestrated by decision makers (although those engaged in peacemaking can systematically influence media content). News items, documentaries, and films that illustrate the predicaments of the Other are vital to peace ecology. Bad news takes care of itself; it is the often-ignored stories of cross-border cooperation and suffering on both sides that the media should seek to amplify.

In June 1997 the Peres Center for Peace, which I founded together with my mentor Shimon Peres, decided to produce a joint Palestinian-Israeli film. We easily found a common theme: stress. The tension that is cultivated during conflict takes its toll on societies on both sides of the divide; it is a common trait, even if it is manifested differently by the two societies. Discussions with the producers, Duki Dror and Rashid Masharawi, and the scriptwriters reminded me of some of the toughest negotiations I had experienced with PLO representatives in Oslo. Both Israeli and Palestinian were trying to outdo each other in their portrayal of the depth of their society's anxieties. Each side wanted to portray itself as the greatest victim, and they downplayed the commonalities of suffering out of fear that their audiences would react negatively to the suggestion that both sides were equally stressed.

After long nights of deliberations, we finally achieved a joint production of two short films. The Palestinian film was mostly silent, depicting jaded faces waiting in humiliation at the blockades between Gaza and Israel. In contrast, the Israeli film was filled with the almost hysterical chatter of a taxi driver to his clients on a day when a suicide bomber killed several people in Jerusalem. Yet a commonality existed between the films—it was clear that anxiety and tension had overcome the people of the region.

The joint production, *Stress,* was broadcast on both Israeli and Palestinian television as well as on international media. Many more such productions might have been created had a film fund or a peace television station been established. But all such efforts are so far in vain. Television, the most critical medium, has not been even partially positioned as a channel for peace.

Regional Influence

The region surrounding the core conflict area can support conflict societies by participating in peacemaking efforts parallel to the central resolution process. Since the end of the Cold War and the consequent cessation of a bipolar global environment, geopolitical unions based on socioeconomic cooperation have been established and continue to develop. In the case of Europe after World War II, countries reconciled into an integrated system, the European Community, which has since been replaced by the European Union. In 1967, the Association of Southeast Asian Nations (ASEAN) was formed to promote political and economic cooperation and regional stability. In the Middle East, however, the 1991 Madrid

Conference launched a regional track to parallel bilateral negotiations but failed to adequately emphasize multilateralism.

National and regional leaders have a great deal of influence in the creation of a peace ecology in conflict societies; they are the most powerful actors of the peace gospel and must use this power to change the existing conflict narrative and the perceptions of the former enemy into a narrative of peace and equality. The political leadership's rhetoric is important—negotiations can be expressed as "us and us" rather than "us and them," for instance, to better promote principles of cooperation and commonality.

In fact, during my first meeting with the PLO in Oslo, we discussed the possibility of a "peace propaganda plan." Our campaign would have focused on relaying a message of *nachnu-anachnu* ("us and us"). Sadly, the concept was never translated into reality by the political leadership, once again demonstrating the need for public leaders to adjust their rhetoric and policies toward supporting a culture of peace. Anwar Sadat was a master at convincing Israelis of his emphatic views regarding their needs; Yasser Arafat was not. A change in rhetoric is a critical requirement for the creation of a peace ecology.

Peace ecology is intimately related to the other three pillars of peacemaking and must be considered at all steps in the peace process. Because it is so intricately linked to the nature of the relationship with the former enemy, its strategies are less tangible and more psychological—making it one of the most difficult, but one of the most crucial, pillars to achieve.

CHAPTER FIVE

Peacebuilding

PEACEBUILDING IS THE POLITICAL, ECONOMIC, AND SOCIAL cooperation and contact between post-conflict societies. When a society progresses from a state of conflict to one of peace, all such cooperation, even at its most banal, must be integral to the process to engender better mutual understanding and work for the common benefit of rehabilitation.

Peacebuilding as a concept can seem abstract—it overlaps with the other pillars in many arenas—but peacebuilding projects are among the most tangible and practical activities in the peacemaking process. Often, peace*building* involves the literal construction of infrastructure—roads, bridges, irrigation, hotels, warehouses, factories, and schools. Sometimes the construction is less tangible —the creation of a fund to assist cross-border soccer teams, for example. In both cases, however, peacebuilding programs are designed to build physical, financial, and political connections where there were none before.

Economic Projects and the Peacebuilding Triangle

Post-conflict economies are generally damaged, if not devastated. Infrastructures have been destroyed and societies lack organized institutions to deal with refugees and displaced people. Security budgets are inflated compared to small social budgets, and governments are often plagued by corruption.

A country's progression from conflict to peace must be reflected in its economy. A war economy must be converted to a peace economy through the creation of necessary, accountable, and transparent institutions to launch the country's rehabilitation. A conflict state's economy is largely determined by its defense establishment, which may contribute to a society's technological know-how but is detrimental to the social fabric of the economy. Peace dividends should germinate from the bottom up, translating to initiatives such as job-intensive megaprojects, advanced social services, and greater equality in the education system.

Three areas that require a great deal of attention from peace-building projects are the rehabilitation of displaced persons, refugees, disabled persons, and child soldiers; the diminishment of socioeconomic gaps through rural-urban integration; and the development of support for children six years old and younger.

Because post-conflict countries must reshape their economies as quickly as possible, most important peace-related decisions concern the intended economic relationships between former enemies and with the international community. The economics of peace-building can be defined as a triangle, with the two countries in conflict on either side and the international community at the triangle's base. Today, the international community deals with conflict countries independently to enhance development and economic growth, but this misses prime opportunities to enhance peace through economic activity that forces former enemies to work directly with each other.

Within the framework of an economic triangle, the international community—particularly the International Monetary Fund (IMF), the World Bank, and the UN Development Programme—can help conflict countries establish joint projects to engender common interests and economic interdependence, and then can create regional and local funding mechanisms to support those projects. The most successful funding programs include substantial earmarking of funds for professional cooperation as well as technical assistance for joint capacity building between former foes. The international community can provide both conflict states with crucial assistance, including micro-infrastructures, feasibility studies, training, marketing, and legislation development, to attract private-sector investment. Free trade agreements—between former enemies and between each of them and the international community, specifically the United States and the European Union—also can be facilitated on an international level. Ultimately, economic borders can enhance security more than barbed wire.

Even during the early days of the fleeting honeymoon at Oslo, no funding (out of approximately $10 billion of assistance funds to both sides) was allocated by the international community for Israeli-Palestinian cooperation. Had 25 percent of these funds been invested in economic cooperation, the whole process might have been different.

Governments are often opposed to such assistance because it does not produce high overhead for donor consultants. But the desires of government bureaucracies do not always align with the needs of post-conflict societies. An economic peace structure should be built to link transportation, energy, water, and investors who previously have not invested in the region because of war. Investment in post-conflict regions is fundamental to sustaining peace.

For instance, joint development of water infrastructure for both drinking and agriculture is fundamental in many post-conflict areas that lack water resources or are suffering from drought. Because conflicts often go hand-in-hand with developmental crises, agricultural development is an important component of joint peacebuilding activities. These activities can include food security projects as well as peri-urban agriculture projects that produce employment in low-income areas.

Health-related peacebuilding projects by their very nature deal with life and the living. Each party can provide different expertise—telemedicine, for example—whereby patients can use hospitals across the conflict border. Doctors and hospital administrators benefit from the exchange of knowledge, and patients benefit from improved access to health care.

Linking cross-border infrastructures—including roads, railways, air and sea routes, energy, water, and so on—can create the physical platform for interconnectivity and cooperation, and it will facilitate the free movement of individuals and commodities. The free movement of people and goods, even if it involves security risks, can only enhance peace and security in the long run.

Peacebuilding projects also can be implemented in specialized border zones comanaged by two or several nations. Tourism zones or other attractions, such as artificial lakes or theme parks for children, can turn the border into a "peace zone." Peacebuilding might include joint industrial zones that provide incentives for investors, including special trade arrangements within and beyond the region. By offering free-trade advantages, qualified industrial zones would distribute both economic and peace dividends.

Shortly after the Peres Center for Peace was established in 1996, the importance of peacebuilding projects became apparent. I realized that such projects were easier to fashion within the environment in which NGOs operate, beyond the rigid bureaucratic peace concepts of government. The Center for Peace provided an outlet for Peres's unique creativity and imagination; we called the Center "Peres's dream factory."

A certain dream-come-true quality was manifest in an agricultural program that we developed with Palestinians, Egyptians, and Israelis. During the summer of 1996, while in Rome, Peres met an intelligent and wealthy forty-year-old entrepreneur named Guido Barilla, also known as the king of pasta production. His company, Barilla, has become the world's leading pasta producer and is a household name in many Western countries.

Peres presented Barilla with a challenge: to grow the wheat for his Italian pasta in the Middle East, where the ecological conditions could be ripe and cost-effective. With Barilla's agreement and the help of a top Israeli agricultural expert, Professor Shmuel Pohoryles, we launched a pilot project to grow wheat in the deserts of Israel, Palestine, and Egypt. To ensure the project would be cost-effective for the Barilla Group, we brought together a group of Israeli, Egyptian, and Palestinian experts to deal with research and development on soil, water, and other elements to yield the necessary durum wheat.

Less than a year later, in the desert-bound region of the Israeli Negev (close to Palestinian Hebron) and in the Egyptian town of Asyūt, known for its fundamentalist population, the project bore fruit—or, more accurately, wheat. That wheat contributed to the production of bread, pasta, and peace. Although the pilot lasted only three years and produced a relatively small amount of wheat, its profits in the peacebuilding department were high. The project, dubbed Pasta for Peace, possessed the key ingredients for peacebuilding: joint negotiations and research, labor and employment for farmers, bread that was produced and consumed in the region, and partnership with a global company. The project fulfilled the needs of peace and development in the region.[1]

The project was celebrated in a ceremony that brought Israelis, Palestinians, Egyptians, and one Italian—Barilla himself—together in the middle of the Negev, among a vast sea of wheat fields. Lands that had been drowned in blood were now flourishing with agriculture; desperation had been replaced with hope in a project that spanned borders and cultures alike. The fundamental goal of peacebuilding—to connect conflict societies in cooperation and creation—had been met.

Tourism

Cross-border tourism is another joint activity that is particularly conducive to peace. Tourism is one of the main mobilization industries actually bringing about a global village; it has the power to bring people closer together, literally and metaphorically. Tourism in post-conflict environments can create cross-border infrastructure such as roads, railways, and open air and sea space. Through cooperative tourism, societies acquire deeper knowledge of one another and can potentially bring large numbers of tourists to lands that were too risky to visit in the past. Tourism also can bring peace dividends to a broad cross section of society, from hotel owners to taxi drivers to bus companies to tour guides, on both sides of the border.

I have long recognized the importance of tourism in peacebuilding, though its potential has been largely ignored in peacemaking circles. In early 1996 I chaired the Israeli delegation during peace negotiations with Syria, at the Wye Plantation outside Washington, DC. The Syrians demanded a full Israeli withdrawal from the Golan Heights, the region Israel occupied in 1967 and that overlooks the whole of northern Israel. In return, the Syrians would agree to normalized and peaceful relations with Israel.

When we asked for Syria's definition of peace, Syrian chief negotiator Walid Mualem, then ambassador to Washington and today Syria's foreign minister, quoted President Hafez al-Assad: "Diplomatic, commercial, and tourism relations." Two prominent groups in my delegation firmly objected to this definition: the defense personnel overseeing security arrangements during peacetime and the lawyers, who named eighteen spheres of normalization, from communication to environment, that had to be included in the peace treaty. (These were based on the Israeli-Egyptian peace treaty; most of the spheres were never implemented.)

Despite their objections, I asked one of the more creative minds of our delegation, Dr. Yossi Vardi, to compose a full peace treaty based mainly on tourism cooperation. We conceived a plan that, following an Israeli withdrawal, would render much of the Golan Heights a tourist zone, with a specific focus on health and ecotourism. The plan included hotel chains on the Heights, complete with roads, energy infrastructure, and special attractions. We planned a worldwide marketing campaign to advertise archeological sites in Syria, Lebanon, and Israel. The large number of monumental sites from antiquity, with their historical and religious significance, would attract a force of tourists that would stabilize peace more than any peacekeeping force.

In partnership with the Syrians, we planned a Mediterranean high road that would link Israel and Europe through Syria and

Lebanon. By driving to Europe, Israelis could purge their feelings of isolation and renounce their national self-perception as a besieged land. To all negotiators' surprise, President al-Assad did not spurn such discussions. On the contrary, he designated Syria's number one hotel developer, Osman Aidi, to deliberate these issues with us and with US private-sector groups led by a prominent Jewish American businessman, Lester Pollack—discussions that did later take place in New York.

Talks with the Syrians collapsed after an outbreak of Palestinian terror in March of that year, which meant that our tourism-based peacebuilding plan could not reach fruition. Still, it remains an important peacebuilding concept for future negotiations because of its great potential for creating stability, strengthening the economy, and encouraging cooperation on both sides of the border.

Technology and the Arts

At its core, peacebuilding is about creating positive effects on people's lives—which also are the stated aims of globalization and the information superhighway. During recent conflicts, affected societies have been deprived of high-tech tools that inspire and connect people and cultures; while these societies have been bogged down by war, the rest of the world has become globalized. People around the world visit the same Web sites, listen to the same music, watch similar feature films, and idolize the same soccer players. The expansion of information technology into post-conflict societies should be an important goal. Much has been said—though little has been done—about closing the digital divide. These infrastructures can be cemented in place by third parties from both the public and the private sectors.

Tools of communication and symbols of globalization can be catalysts for change; they can penetrate post-conflict societies and inspire the younger generation. Information technology can contribute quantitatively and qualitatively to the peace process. On the same note, the international community should not tolerate countries such as Syria that heavily monitor Internet usage. Information technology and peacebuilding industries should be used in conjunction to create a sense of belonging, a common language, and ongoing interaction between former enemies.

Other industries integral to peacebuilding include the arts, entertainment, and sports. Following conflict, former enemies lack a common language, so potential dialogue is hampered by prejudice and stereotypes. The arts can overcome communication barriers through the establishment of film and music studios, theaters, and joint work based on cultural expression and exchange. The mainstream media often focuses on the detriments of peace processes, so it is important to employ other joint media opportunities, such as film, to present positive developments. As a result, a common language will evolve and foster mutual understanding.

Youth Projects

In post-conflict societies, children may be young in age but not in experience. Many youth that have lived through violent conflict have been traumatized by war—they suffer from deep emotional scars that are not easily healed. Many young people, eighteen years old and younger, are perceived to be mature and strong enough to be employed as soldiers during conflict—to fight, to kill, and to be killed. It should be obvious, then, that these young people are also old enough to work with their former enemies toward a modern, participatory peace.

Sports can have an enormous impact on the well-being of youth by providing an important outlet for personal expression, contributing to a sense of belonging, and allowing children to behave as children—as they are generally unable to do during conflict. Most conflict countries lack soccer fields, basketball courts, gymnastic equipment, and swimming pools. As the basis of any rehabilitation process, the international community must invest in these infrastructures and initiate joint activities, training, and competitions among youth on both sides of the conflict.

During the summer of 1999 the Vatican's ambassador to the Holy Land invited me to participate in a most surprising peacebuilding project. With the blessing of the Holy See, he suggested that, in conjunction with a Palestinian NGO (led by the courageous peace fighter Kamel Husseini) and Italian NGOs, we organize a soccer game. The game was to be held in Rome's Olympic stadium and would pit a team comprising pop singers and worldrenowned Italian soccer stars against a joint Israeli-Palestinian soccer team chosen from the best players in both Israel and the Palestinian Authority. The teams would be spiced up with a sprinkle of Hollywood and sports stars; spectators would include the president of Italy, Shimon Peres, and Yasser Arafat.

After long preparations and unconventional negotiations with Arafat in May 1999, sixty thousand people filled the Stadio Olimpico. Teams competed as planned and included Sean Connery, the soccer legend Pelé, and Michael Schumacher, the Formula 1 world champion. In addition to the 5-4 win for the first-ever Israeli-Palestinian joint team, the game had two other important results: it was transmitted live in both countries—illustrating that when former enemies appear together, the world takes note—and the income generated from tickets was used to build soccer and computer infrastructures in schools on both sides of the border.

Today, using a half million dollars provided by the tickets and the international community, Israel and Palestine have twenty-four twin schools playing soccer and a joint indoor soccer team made up of Israeli and Palestinian players, which has won the Israeli indoor soccer championship. In 2002, the Israeli-Palestinian team played a Rwandan team that included Hutus and Tutsis.

To some, such events may seem anecdotal. But for the youth who participate in the project, soccer changes their attitudes toward the Other more than any governmental policy initiative could. I had a vision of covering all Israeli and Palestinian cities with green fields of peace—soccer fields, that is. Implementation has been limited so far, but there is always hope.

Peacebuilding must be activated in all arenas that affect the attitudes and motivations of former enemies. Ultimately, the goal of peacebuilding is to present cooperation with former enemies as legitimate and beneficial. Although peacebuilding activities should be implemented among many groups—including security forces, businesspeople, physicians, and soccer stars—I believe that peacebuilding should emphasize youth. Their openness and enthusiasm allow them to respond positively to cross-border activities—and when they become empowered, they can serve as engines for broader change in their societies.

CHAPTER SIX

Creative Diplomacy

FEW POLITICAL ACTIVITIES ARE SO MISUNDERSTOOD AND underestimated as diplomacy. It is often seen as a behavioral pattern rather than the pursuit of national interests and peace. Calling a person "diplomatic" has come to be almost an insult—it is parochially perceived, at best, as not being candid and, at worst, as being deceitful. Diplomats themselves have often misinterpreted its real usefulness. As the author Daniele Vare said, "Diplomacy is the art of letting someone have your way."

But one-sided solutions merely provoke the losing side to want to overturn the situation. Creative diplomacy invites us to view compromise as a positive opportunity rather than a potential loss. By concentrating on innovating solutions that emphasize how *both sides* will gain, we can tackle complicated problems with flexibility and mutual respect.

If militant methods are the heart of warmaking, then creative diplomacy must be the heart of peacemaking. In war, diplomacy serves the interests of the war effort. In peace, security must be geared toward peacemaking and maneuvered by diplomacy. Too often, peacemakers treat security as a means to achieve peace, but it should be the other way around. Only peace can achieve security. Security must be perceived in its broadest and most comprehensive sense; it should not simply be highlighted as a bone of contention but should provide citizens with a feeling of safety in the long run. Through creative diplomacy, peacemakers can steer the security situation toward guaranteed calm, employing security steps such as demilitarization, security coordination, weapons control, and external monitoring to prevent a new flare-up.

Creative diplomacy aims to explore and express common interests that can evolve into practical peacebuilding projects. Creativity should not result in unrealistic promises; diplomatic activity must always be realistic and accountable. This kind of creativity relies on leadership. As Sir John Hoskyns put it, "Strategic leadership requires ... a readiness to look personally foolish; a readiness to discuss half-baked ideas, since most fully baked ideas start out in that form."[1] Leaders that are appropriate to peace diplomacy possess a character that is generous, magnanimous, forgiving, and uncompromising when it comes to basic humanitarian values. Creative diplomacy implemented by the right leaders is a bridge to peace in all its facets.

I have been party to many small-scale efforts at creative diplomacy. For example, in July 1994 Israelis and Palestinians negotiated a historic agreement to transfer parts of the West Bank territory and authority to the Palestinians. The agreement also implied the first free and fair election of the Palestinian Authority's chairman and parliament.

Every detail of these elections was negotiated, including the participation of Palestinians living in East Jerusalem, which was the most contentious issue at the time. Under the agreement, Jerusalem would not fall under the Palestinian Authority's jurisdiction of the West Bank and Gaza. However, we took into consideration that under no circumstances would Arafat and his team hold elections without East Jerusalemites being eligible to vote.

Although we understood the nature of their predicament, the Israeli delegation was opposed to holding elections in East Jerusalem in the same manner as they were going to be held in the West Bank and Gaza, because the elections could affect the city's status in a similar way.

My Palestinian counterpart Abu Ala and I knew that we alone could not resolve this issue and that there would be repercussions regarding the future status of Jerusalem. Together with Chairman Arafat and Foreign Minister Peres, we were invited to Cairo by

Egyptian President Hosni Mubarak to be part of a very creative exercise in diplomacy.

The Israeli side favored the idea that East Jerusalemite Palestinians would vote like Palestinians abroad—through an absentee ballot. However, the Palestinians wanted to mirror election practices in the West Bank and Gaza by setting up voting stations. After intense backroom discussions, President Mubarak thought up a most creative solution to our problem. Polling stations would be set up inside East Jerusalem post offices for the duration of the election. Israelis could claim the Palestinians were sending their votes by mail as absentee ballots, whereas the Palestinians could assert that East Jerusalemites were voting in regular polling stations that happened to be at post offices. All that was left was a creative design that reconciled a post box and a polling booth—an easy hurdle once everyone was on board.

In the end, both sides got what they wanted without having to sacrifice their fundamental needs and ideals. Granted, many challenges of modern peacemaking are more complicated than casting ballots. But if we approach these contentions with creative diplomacy in mind, we can frame compromises as gains for all.

The decision to make peace is not enough to prevent devastating war. Peacemaking efforts must address the core beliefs and activities of society and its leaders. This new peace architecture rests on the four pillars: participatory peace and glocalization, peace ecology, peacebuilding, and creative diplomacy.

But how do we create this structure? What are the steps to creating a "modern" peace? This is the subject of part 3.

PART III

The Modern Process

Steps to Lasting Peace

INTRODUCTION

The Modern Process

NEARLY ALL PEACEMAKING TODAY TAKES PLACE BEHIND CLOSED doors. Small groups of diplomats and leaders gather in private settings to produce documents that are supposed to represent the interests of many. Even if that elite group understands the value of the four pillars of modern peace, however, avoiding the traps of historical treaties requires actively building the peacemaking process on those modern ideals.

Glocalization, peace ecology, peacebuilding, and creative diplomacy emphasize the civilian aspects of peacemaking and are therefore a natural progression in its evolution. Part 3 explains how these four pillars need to be the foundation on which peace is planned, negotiated, and built. Rather than presenting the modern process as one size fits all, I have tried to present the conditions and approaches that, in my experience and studies, provide the greatest potential to build lasting, sustainable peace from the ground up. In other words, although I hope to see my specific recommendations put into action, the more important point is the reasoning behind these recommendations. I recognize that governments and cultures operate according to different perceptions and methods; I believe that the principles behind the modern process can offer positive guidance for any conflict-resolution situation, anywhere.

This section is not written merely for professional peacemakers, as a blueprint for the modern process; it also is an attempt to throw open the closed doors of peacemaking and to invite the scrutiny and participation of the greater society. By making the process more transparent, I hope to give citizens a way to engage more directly with peacemaking. The modern process must not be a series of secretive encounters but an open and welcoming approach, involving the interaction of two societies in addition to two negotiating teams. Citizens will have the opportunity to communicate their unique needs, and those at the helm of the process will have the opportunity both to support and to depend on the populations they represent.

The road to peace is never a straight line, but as long as we are guided by the principles of the four pillars we can at least keep ourselves pointed in the right direction.

CHAPTER SEVEN

The Peace Barometer

WE ARE A WORLD OBSESSED WITH MEASUREMENTS. ENTIRE industries are dedicated to tracking vast varieties of economic data, from the Nasdaq to unemployment, inflation to interest rates. Although quantifying economic growth and decline is valuable, such figures tell us little about the true state of society. To assess that, there are organizations that measure literacy or infant mortality rates—there's even a push for indexing Gross National Happiness[1]—but when was the last time these figures were displayed prominently on the local news?

It is time to move social and psychological measurements to the forefront of our evaluations of the state of society, particularly when it comes to peace. When a society moves from war to peace, economic data tells only half the story; other measurements are necessary to evaluate the psychological state of society. As I discussed in chapter 4 on peace ecology, economic indicators make no difference if a population's mind-set is stuck within a culture of war.

Sustainable peace relies on the attitudes and cooperation of the people who have lived with conflict. To effect a genuine change in conflict and post-conflict societies, people must choose peaceful settlement and cooperation, advocate compromise for potential gain, support regional integration, and embrace the international community and multiculturalism without abandoning local traditions—all by free will, not by force. Peace must be accepted and valued by societies, in action as well as in word.

But the definition of the word *peace* is not absolute; people perceive peace differently according to their own definitions and cultural perceptions. Differing definitions of peace can lead to dissatisfaction, frustration, conflict, and violence within societies and across borders. It is impossible to form an objective picture of a population's views of peace because leaders usually speak on behalf of the public and the media echoes those sentiments. Elections, which do not take place very frequently in democratic societies, let alone in nondemocratic ones, give only a vague idea of voters' opinions.

Therefore, before any other part of the peacemaking process begins, research must be undertaken to measure the conflict societies' attitudes toward peace—how they define peace, what they want out of a peace agreement, and how they view current approaches to local and regional conflict resolution. Such data can help decision makers acquire as objective a view as possible of the range of opinion and can steer peacemaking toward a course that fulfills the needs of the silent majority.

Measuring Peace

Similar to the way the Nasdaq measures stocks, a "peace barometer" can be used to measure public opinion in countries that want to liberate themselves from a state of conflict. A peace barometer can identify the social impetus toward peace and the primary opposition to it; these measurements can be used by governments, NGOs, and civil organizations to better direct policy and approaches to the peacemaking process.

The peace barometer allows us to study the role of psychological processes and attitudes in violence and peacebuilding—for example, the differentiation between "us" and "them." We can study the effects of victimization and the ways in which it inhibits empathy for the Other and makes the world seem dangerous. Relations between groups are greatly affected by culture, societal institutions, and political processes; the peace barometer helps us identify these intersections and understand how they can be influenced toward peaceful values.

In late 2005 the Peres Center for Peace worked with Gallup International to survey Israeli and Palestinian attitudes toward peace. This project (the partial results of which are included in part 4 in the context of the Pax Mediterraneo) helped us identify the core values and beliefs on each side, which influenced our organizational approach to peacebuilding. Polling in this region continues on an ongoing basis, capturing perpetually changing attitudes.

Peace barometers elsewhere can be modeled on the structure initiated by the Peres Center for Peace, which employs both qualitative and quantitative methods to measure populations' perceptions and beliefs. Instead of blanket surveys that focus on a few broad questions, the peace barometer uses face-to-face interviews to explore people's attitudes in depth. These interviews, lasting approximately an hour each, are conducted with random samples of citizens to gain an overall range of public opinions.

The questions in the Middle Eastern peace barometer are divided into six categories: war and peace, vision and identity, creative diplomacy, economic cooperation, the role of the international community, and peace ecology. These categories and the specific questions can be tailored for individual conflicts, depending on the regional situation and the stage of the peace process. All peace barometer surveys can be designed to measure the public's attitude toward the culture of peace; the benefits of peace; the United States, the European Union, the United Nations, or another international peace-brokering presence; Western culture; and possible social mobilization—for example, the willingness of people to participate in peace projects, and the value of peace education.

The data collected from these surveys make it possible to evaluate the impact of peacebuilding initiatives at both a micro level (domestic politics) and a macro level (regional politics), thereby promoting systematic research and thinking about issues connected with peacemaking and conflict resolution.

Within any society that moves from conflict to peace there remain forces that would rather continue the conflict. These groups are often driven by religious figures who exploit a fertile ground of poverty to recruit weak and disgruntled populations to extreme, militant, nationalistic, and often obtuse viewpoints. It's easy for conflict populations to fall in love with the conflict culture because it is convenient to abdicate responsibility for one's own misery and instead to blame the enemy. It's also easy for the media to focus only on these negative groups and thus to perpetuate the belief that each side is still trapped in a culture of conflict.

The peace barometer can identify the negative elements in a society, but it also can bring to light the silent majority that favors peace processes and coexistence. Governments, NGOs, and civil societies can emphasize these positive groups and help transform this passive majority to an active majority within the framework of the modern participatory peace.

CHAPTER EIGHT

Peacemakers

THE TERM *peacemaker* HAS TRADITIONALLY BEEN APPLIED ONLY to those who are directly involved in the planning, negotiation, and signing of a peace treaty. This definition is very limiting. In our modern peace, every member of society—both in the conflict states and in neighboring countries—has the ability to contribute to peace.

Of course, there is only so much room around the negotiating table. There is a clear gap between the ideals of participatory peace and the practical demands of the peacemaking process—a gap that can be bridged by new perceptions about who can be a peacemaker and on what level. In this chapter I offer new definitions of the terms *peace leader* and *peace bureaucrat*. The former occupy a highly visible role in the peacemaking process; the latter represent a more diverse group of actors in government, nongovernmental organizations, and the public and private sectors. Peace bureaucrats are the link between the elite negotiating team and the greater society; they help communicate the needs of society to the peace leaders and explain the actions of peace leaders to their constituencies. Understanding the unique characteristics and responsibilities of peace leaders and peace bureaucrats will be crucial to shaping the modern peace process for the benefit of all.

The Peace Leader

Dedicated and open-minded political leadership is crucial to peacemaking. The main qualities of a peace leader are vision, courage, character, and integrative capacities. Peace leaders must possess a clear direction for the future; too many political leaders are over-ly cautious about preventing the mistakes of the past. Leaders that are endlessly preoccupied with the previous war cannot lead a pro-cess toward future peace. A peace leader must be hypnotized by the future—a future that goes beyond the date of the next elections.

A peace revolution can only transpire when conventional wisdom is shunned and the status quo is altered. This revolution requires courage. Peacemaking is about strategic decisions and compromise, but compromising with an enemy is often interpreted as weakness. In the sphere of peacemaking, leaders who concentrate on cultivat-ing strategic ingenuity and imagination will have the best chance of contributing to successful negotiations. A peace architect for the future creates solutions out of nonexistent "materials."

The most useful career experience for the peacemaking leader is difficult to define. Given the flaws of traditional peacemaking, a background in security is generally not desired and definitely is insufficient. The temptation to import the use of power into future strategic considerations is too dangerous.

A fundamental understanding of people is critical to under-standing the needs of populations on both sides of the conflict bor-der. Modern peace is about the hearts and minds of people, not maps and borders, and social empathy is therefore an important characteristic for a peace leader.

Experience in trade unions or local government is useful, and peace leaders such as Charles de Gaulle of France, David Ben-Gurion of Israel, and Mustafa Kemal Atatürk of Turkey all had experience in trade unions,[1] which contributed to the empathy that later guided their peacemaking endeavors.

In political life, peace is often divided among the relevant sec-tions of government, including security, economy, foreign affairs, and infrastructure. The peacemaker at the helm will increase the chances of a successful peace process if he or she understands the relevance of peace to each of these sectors and provides an inte-grated and diversified approach that includes the various elements of peace. We can think of peace leaders as teachers, guiding public opinion toward peace by modeling peaceful values. With the support of peace leaders, the public can learn to see the advantages of compromise and to view the former enemy in a different light. The ecological role of the peacemaker is indispensable to creating a participatory peace process.

Based on the concepts of peace ecology and peacebuilding, a peace leader leads the way in making critical decisions and in monitoring negotiations, treaties, and treaty implementation. He or she has the opportunity to emphasize cooperative ventures and inspire an atmosphere of peace. The best leaders are filled with a passion for peace and the patience to realize it.

Because the necessary attributes for leaders are difficult to come by in one person, a very small group of individuals—the peace leaders—can lead the peace process and thus draw on a greater depth of collective knowledge. A small group also can be better than a large group at protecting the discretion of internal deliberations.

For Once, In Praise of Bureaucrats

Peace leaders, whether as individuals or in small groups, do not act independently. Alongside the political elite stands the peace army—officials of the relevant government ministries, heads of NGOs, businesspeople, and civil leaders—and when it comes to the bureaucracy, the more warriors involved in the peace process, the better. These are the peace bureaucrats, the people who have the ability to connect the high ideals of peace leaders with the policy changes and peacebuilding programs that affect the society at large. Rather than thinking of bureaucracy as a red tape nightmare, we can think of it as an opportunity to bring as many players as possible into the peacemaking process.

During wartime, an army defends the state. Conflict prevents government officials from working with the other side, often a neighbor, and this division severely limits operations within a regional context. Part of making the transition from conflict to peace is reestablishing cross-border relationships. A training program can greatly improve the capacity of officials to work across borders and to overcome any legalities that previously prevented cooperation. Projects can be initiated by relevant officials, and project managers can be chosen according to their capacity to implement projects. In this way the relationships needed to implement joint socioeconomic projects will be created.

In times of war, society is co-opted to contribute to the national agenda; during conflict resolution, societies should be given a similar opportunity to contribute to the realization of peace. From this perspective, each citizen can be a peacemaker and can contribute to the spectrum of values needed to strategically activate a society. Three major actors can be recruited to fulfill this mission: NGOs, local governments of cities with active civil societies, and the private sector. These actors form the foundation of glocalization—local and global players cooperating and the home front providing global opportunities.

Nongovernmental organizations, both international and local, are important players in a modernized peace. *Non* is the pivotal idea here—NGOs are driven by values, operating almost anarchically, with much energy and with relatively few resources, for the betterment of society. It is well known that a substantial percentage of foreign aid has moved from governments to NGOs in the past twenty years. Although many organizations act in diverse and uncoordinated ways, together they form a family. When their operations are geared toward peace and financed by governments, they can function in a kind of "orchestrated anarchy" as an enormous driving force for peace.

Peace NGOs should be led by strategically minded individuals so that their modular projects are later multiplied and sustainable. NGOs will have a greater chance of impact when they are staffed by imaginative, creative, and audacious young people; the value of experience is generally overrated, and the peace and development experience is often nothing more than frustrating. Young people have the ability to think outside the box and tend to believe that anything is possible. Experience, on the other hand, generally provides brilliant reasons why an endeavor is impossible. A peace revolution depends on the belief that, with the right approach, we can make the seemingly impossible possible.

Local government is another important anchor in the participatory process, because of its proximity to its constituency and its social orientation. As I have noted in my discussion of glocalization, mayors can be modern-day peacemakers. If peace both today and tomorrow is dependent on its acceptance and absorption by societies, mayors—thanks to today's accelerated urbanization—are closest to city residents and best understand their needs. To become peacemakers, mayors from conflict areas can create networks with cross-border cities and external third cities that can lend capacities and resources and can cooperate within an intercity peace relationship.

City-to-city relationships can provide a forum of exchange about issues of concern to the daily lives of citizens, such as sewage, urban planning, tourism, cultural exchange, and youth exchange—in other words, about every subject that can enhance the peace of the citizenry. This focus on everyday needs can ensure that peace dividends trickle down to the civilian masses. Mayors can recruit for this campaign various elements in local civil societies. Increased cooperation between cities means greater stability, the potential for multiculturalism, and more opportunities for economic growth on both sides of the border.

Professionals, organizations, and businesses also should be motivated to link up with their peers across the conflict border. Hospitals can work with hospitals and schools can work with schools, sports clubs can compete against one another, cultural institutions can exchange works, and universities can cooperate on research. Imagine the cultural and educational institutions of Washington, DC, working with those of Baghdad; it paints a very different picture than is created by having only the cities' governments working together. And just like that, doctors, artists, and engineers can become modern-day peacemakers, linking up with their colleagues to cooperate and build peace. In such a scenario, everyone benefits from the exchange of knowledge and experience. Both sides improve their technical capacities and, in the process, promote mutual understanding and respect.

The private sector constitutes the last group of peace bureaucrats. With the impetus of the free market economy and globalization in recent decades, much of the world's capital has moved from the public to the private sector. Many global companies post annual sales numbers that are far larger than the gross national product of most countries in the world.[2] But global wealth brings with it a global responsibility.

The central goal of all corporations is to make more money than their competitors—and when corporations invest in peace, profits will follow. Corporate social responsibility—business organizations' contribution to their communities—is good for citizens and good for business. Peace is rife with socially responsible opportunities for the private sector; it is a sphere to which the private sector can contribute, through its economic growth and through direct contributions to the peace process. Investing in peace will bring greater stability to previously risky regions and thus will increase chances for profit—new markets for goods, services, and reconstruction. Citizens and corporations alike can benefit from economic growth in post-conflict societies.

The international private sector can contribute to peace by lending capacities to the public and private sectors in post-conflict areas, helping to create an environment conducive to investment. The private sector also can create private-public partnerships that favor regional development and lead to investment in the new peace economy.

Although peace champions from the private sector are few, they possess a broader vision of their role in society and the world and don't perceive their contribution to peace as charity. They recognize that international stability is in their interest and in the interests of their shareholders.

The greater goal is to create a peacemakers' web that connects responsible peace leaders, peace bureaucrats, and civilian peacemakers in rhetoric, policies, and grassroots peacebuilding activities. The transition toward decentralization will be difficult but ultimately beneficial for all parties involved. Peace cannot simply be governed and absorbed by the elite; it must be a participatory process that allows the needs of citizens to intersect with the needs of government, NGOs, and corporations.

CHAPTER NINE

Planning

THE BEST PEACE TREATIES STEM FROM THOROUGH PREPARATION combined with a sense of flexibility and spontaneity. The people involved in this planning stage are the same small group of peace leaders that is described in chapter 8—though the concepts in this chapter can also apply to NGOs, private companies, and civil organizations that are preparing to establish relationships with counterparts across the border. The various peace leaders can be assigned to working teams that address political leadership, planning, negotiating, peacebuilding, and peace ecology, with local government units, civil society players, and private-sector groups participating.

The planning stage must not be taken lightly. Establishing goals and expectations at the outset reduces the chance of surprises and deal breakers later in the negotiations—thus contributing to a stronger, more solid peace agreement.

Strategic Goals

The beginning of war is often all too obvious: a bomb, a battle, a deployment of troops. Defining the start of peace is far more difficult. Often, those involved in the planning stages of a peace process continue with a conflict mind-set; negotiations begin without defining ultimate goals because the goal seems obvious: peace. But failing to define the strategic objectives of a peace process is a mistake. Goals should not be defined in terms of the best outcome of the peace treaty but in terms of a strategic situation that has both the optimal benefits for both sides and the greatest chance of sustainability. In peace, the object should not be to defeat the former opponent but to allow both parties to gain.

Long-term goal planning should include the creation of an "architectural plan" for the future that takes into consideration all relevant elements. The planning of long-term goals demands courageous decisions about political and social aims that may touch the very identity of nations. Peace generally instigates a movement toward a more liberal and open identity as physical and emotional borders open up. Simultaneously, the interests of the other side must be understood, to plan a reasonable compromise that will satisfy both parties and possibly their global and regional partners.

The New Peace Partner

Deciphering the needs and mentality of the new partner can prove difficult because the partner is also in a transitional process of defining its interests and goals. Still, a transformation in the national perception of the partner is integral. When peace leaders replace the concept of "enemy" with the concept of "partner," they can bring about a similar change in public opinion—an integral element in shifting from a war ecology to a peace ecology.

The traditional means of applying historical lessons and information from intelligence services often have been misleading. The use of historical experience to determine the future is not an objective measurement but an interpretation. History can be defined as the prediction of the past, but expertise about the past does not engender an expert opinion about the future.

Furthermore, intelligence services have become the main vehicle for understanding and prophesying the interests and maneuvers of the former enemy. This reliance on intelligence services can be especially dangerous during the transition from war to peace. Today we can receive precise if partial information about a nation and can hear the private and public rhetoric of political leaders, but we have no way of assessing what is in the minds of leaders when they approach a dynamic situation. Intelligence may be operational when time stands still, but it can rarely assess change. For example, neither the Israeli internal services nor the Western intelligence agencies predicted the revolutionary change of Egypt's President Sadat coming to Jerusalem and offering peace in 1977.

A much safer and better way to understand the former enemy in the new role as a peace partner is simply to listen during meetings and negotiations. Although some fiction may surface, over time the facts prevail. Another method of appreciating the partner is to endeavor to grasp its environment, myths, and opinions; this can only happen through direct contact with the people, the place, and the media. In this context, open sources are superior to and safer than covert sources; we can more easily view and appreciate needs and interests in a dynamic cultural setting. Such understanding leads to the manufacture of a language that may make the parties more comprehensible and trustworthy to one another, enabling them to begin to think of solutions together.

Erecting the Four Pillars

To ensure that a peace treaty rests on the four pillars of modern peace, leaders can use the planning stage to discuss opportunities for incorporating glocalization, peace ecology, peacebuilding, and creative diplomacy into the agreement. Such a discussion acknowledges in a formal setting the value of the four pillars and reassures peace bureaucrats that they, too, will have a great deal of responsibility in peacemaking.

Even at the outset it is essential to coordinate with the other side the cultivation of a peace ecology; words and pictures transcend borders. The political, pedagogical line on the importance of peace needs to be predefined; those who interact with public opinion must determine a basic line of argument in this area. The media is a crucial channel for amplifying a peace campaign. Leaders can plan the arguments and interviews that will spread the gospel of peace. These campaigns should be jointly planned and should avoid a race to recruit the media and score points during negotiations, which would only turn the sides against each other and poison the atmosphere.

Much lip service is wasted on the prosperity that comes with peace. This wealth does not simply fall from heaven. Economic planning in relation to each side's national budget is crucial and generally is underestimated. The movement from a war economy to a peace economy is a transition that creates new budgetary priorities, including the gradual reduction of defense budgets and the strengthening of funding for infrastructure, social rehabilitation, and educational opportunities. New trade targets must be located and investment-friendly projects must be facilitated. Future economic relations with the peace partner must be planned on the basis of economic forecasts on both sides, serving as a foundation for increased regional economic development. Private-sector leaders can contribute a great deal to this economic planning.

It is also useful to identify other peacebuilding areas that will require cooperation, including culture, sports, health, agriculture, technology, and urban issues. Such cooperation does not come naturally and must be formally recognized as an important condition for a successful peace. The participation of local government leaders and NGOs in this part of the planning stage will open the process to a wider coalition of peacemakers, which can represent the needs of citizens with greater accuracy than can elite peace leaders alone.

Planning is, in its way, a sort of negotiation, which is why creative diplomacy can be especially useful. It is not difficult to identify the stumbling blocks that will create major crises between parties. But instead of each side imagining its own vision of the future and the elements on which it will not compromise, both can focus their energy on thinking of creative solutions to problems of the past. Such forward thinking will help smooth out potential blocks in negotiations and will ensure a more efficient and effective agreement.

Peace processes tend to be crisis-ridden, with both time and goodwill squandered over historical stumbling blocks. Creative diplomacy can provide imaginative solutions in which both sides feel that they've won.

CHAPTER TEN

Negotiation

IN THE SUMMER OF 1999 MY GOOD FRIEND JAN STEINBECK,[1] with whom I cofounded the Glocal Forum, invited me and my main Palestinian negotiating partner from the Oslo Accords, Abu Ala, to give a seminar on negotiations to approximately one hundred CEOs, mostly Americans, in Da Nang, Vietnam. The seminar was proof of the futility of conflict. Israeli and PLO officials deliberated negotiating tactics with the Americans and the Vietnamese. Hypothetically speaking, if a time machine could have taken us back forty years, hundreds of thousands of lives might have been spared.

I recall saying to Abu Ala, "It took three thousand hours to negotiate the existing Oslo agreements. It will take many more to negotiate the future ones. If we could theoretically create a piece of computer software that would tabulate the interests of both sides into perfect agreements in one day, would you do it?" Abu Ala answered with an emphatic no. He believed that one needs time for ideas to percolate, to adapt to compromises, to embrace all issues. Negotiation is a transitional period in conflict resolution, during which each side gets the chance to understand the other and itself. Those around the negotiating table can be role models for the rest of society by embodying the peaceful values of trust, openness, and mutual respect.

Negotiators fall under our new definition of peace leaders, which means they have the opportunity and the responsibility to infuse negotiations with the modern peace values of equality, dignity, and democratization. The role of negotiators is to represent the interests of their populations, which often means balancing immediate needs with long-term regional goals. Achieving this balance requires several key qualities that, when present in negotiators, improve the chances of successfully negotiating a modern peace treaty.

The Characteristics of a Modern Negotiator

Some people are born negotiators; children are our best example —no one can be more adamant than a child, and among themselves they often compromise, too. But the choice of negotiators is important and should not depend on the shrewdness of the individual alone. Leaders have the chance to advance modern peace by identifying men and women who possess a strategic perspective on peacemaking, who are independent and active thinkers, who know how to listen and invoke trust. In addition, they must be deal makers, not merely people who are good at befriending. And yes, negotiators also must be tough—mentally and physically—to endure the test of lengthy negotiations.

It is important to choose negotiators who communicate well on an interpersonal basis, because informal talks are equal to more formal ones. Interpersonal relations create a valuable chemistry between teams. Negotiators should be blessed with a good sense of humor, which is a sign of perspective and self-criticism—two important traits during deliberations. Humor is a particular asset in the beginning of negotiations; it helps break the ice and create a common language where there is none. Finally, negotiators must know how to insist on the primary issues and to sophisticatedly compromise on secondary issues. They must possess a strategy regarding the equations of interests between the parties.

The political leadership must build a team of individuals with these inherent qualities and with various other areas of expertise, placing the most suitable person at its helm. This person must have the full confidence of the leadership and also be a good team leader.

The preparation of the negotiation team is important—negotiations include both strategic and tactical aspects and it is important to prepare for both. Strategic aspects are linked to the vision of peace and thus pertain to the preparation of strategic goals and their intersection with the perceived interests of the other side. Tactical aspects relate to the text, the "battle," and the distribution of roles within the team.

It is absolutely critical that negotiators have a constant open line to decision makers and that the chief negotiator has the ear and trust of the head executive. With the decision makers, the negotiators must keep their eyes on the desired plan for peace, because during negotiations there is no issue too small to dwell on for weeks on end. A narrow focus can divert attention away from the goals, especially when the negotiations begin to look like a boxing match. Modernized peace necessitates joint strategizing based on mutual understanding, which can contribute to the sustainability of peace.

Shimon Peres was once asked whether he better understood the Palestinian people after hundreds of hours of negotiations. He replied, "I am not sure, but I definitely better understand human beings." This insight into human relationships is a prerequisite for peace.

Modern Strategy

Negotiations will have the greatest chance of bringing about a modernized peace agreement if the teams are structured to focus specifically on the four pillars of modern peace. For example, one group could deal with the core political issues that are the stumbling blocks of conflict resolution—the issues that demand the most creative diplomacy. A second group could deal with peacebuilding, including economic and social issues, and outline in great detail the type and essence of peacebuilding projects. Group three could deal with the international system, representing the interests of both sides; this should include issues of aid, international peacekeepers, and international guarantees. Group four would concentrate on implementation and monitoring issues; detailed implementation across the board is the key to success. A fifth group, advised by the heads of the delegation, could handle drafting, so that drafting does not become an issue that holds up the deliberative end of the negotiation. Group six would deal with the public relations that contribute to the cultivation of a peace ecology (this issue could be tackled in conjunction with the third group, so negotiations don't degenerate into a media war). Finally, a seventh group could be created from among the heads of the delegation committee, who have a common handle on the negotiations and can assure the basic joint strategy. This group would resolve some of the more difficult issues. Messages could be passed to and from the political leaders, which would allow the chief negotiators to strategize together and make progress.

One strategic part of negotiation is tone. Modern negotiations include the opportunity to engage in both formal and informal, open dialogue about the strategic goals of the negotiation. This dialogue can be framed in terms of creative diplomacy, focusing on the fact that the negotiations are working toward an agreement that will benefit both sides—a balance of interests and not a balance of forces. Open discussion of the regional strategic reality in the aftermath of the agreement will be crucial to acknowledging the practical difficulties facing negotiators and the challenges of implementing a peace agreement. Defining the role of the key international players also will help pave the way for smoother, more effective implementation. In addition, frank and open discussions regarding the predicaments of each side in relation to internal politics and public opinion will help define the contours of a feasible strategic agreement, including diplomatic, peacebuilding, and peace ecology elements.

Modern peace relies on mutual trust and understanding—two important components that can be reflected in negotiations. During the negotiating process, there is much bluffing, especially regarding the deadlines of negotiations. Concessions are "sold" at a higher price than their real value. This is a normal and legitimate part of a negotiation game. But trust must prevail between partners at critical moments in the negotiations—particularly when it comes to making decisions about critical issues in the final stages. Modern peace must be built on modern values.

Toward the final stages of negotiations on Oslo II, late in the summer of 1995, for instance, my mother had just passed away. Abu Ala came to visit my parents' home—a moving gesture in the midst of heavy negotiations. I showed him my late father's library and presented him with an old Koran with a red cover that my father had bought in Cairo in the 1940s.

When we met again in Eilat, Israel, we decided to finalize with Ambassador Dennis Ross a deadline that would be acceptable to President Clinton. It was critical that Abu Ala and I trust each other if we were to resolve the outstanding issues before the deadline was up. Throughout the negotiations, I had been meeting with him every night at midnight in his small suite. His table was always filled with piles of papers from the many working committees we had established.

One night, after the deadline was set, I again entered his room at midnight. The living room was empty. His messy table was cleared of all papers and covered with a white cloth. On it he had placed the red Koran of my father. Then he entered the room, dressed in a traditional white jalabya. He sat opposite me and said in a serious voice, "Now we can finish our business." He had given me the sign that I could trust him and that he trusted me. That night we resolved thirty of the forty outstanding issues in the negotiations. Our trust and faith guided us toward an agreement that would bring the fruits of peace to both sides in equal measure.

Another critical issue that can be reframed in terms of modern peace involves the future relationship between the parties. Instead of only solving problems of the past, negotiations have the opportunity to build bridges to the future. By coming to a mutual understanding about the long-term relationship between the two parties, partners can focus on the topics that need to be resolved and structured to reach that cooperative vision.

Also important is the presence or absence of mediators. In my experience and studies, bilateral negotiations offer the best opportunity for former enemies to hammer out compromises and engage in cooperative peacebuilding. A process that includes a third party induces the two interlocutors to try to convince the mediator and not each other. On the other hand, the difficulty and frustration of working directly with the other side is a fundamental part of turning enemies into partners.

Tactics

This is one of the few areas that requires little change from the methods of traditional peace processes. First and foremost, participants on both sides must be good, professional negotiators or an unequal agreement may come about. Participants must be tough and must be good team players, capable of discreet brainstorming. People who cannot be totally discreet should not even be considered for negotiations.

It also is important to keep the contents of negotiations themselves confidential until agreement. If compromises are leaked before agreement, without quid pro quo, they will become virtually impossible to achieve. Discretion does not necessarily mean a closed-door approach; it simply means knowing which elements of negotiation are best shared with the media, to contribute to positive coverage, and which elements are best kept close until a final agreement has been reached.

Perhaps the most important negotiation is between each team and its home base. Those who remain at home—often political leaders—see themselves as perfect negotiators, because they only negotiate with themselves and don't have to confront the opposition. It is important that the negotiation team reports regularly and honestly about difficulties and does not portray itself as heroes. The political elite must be told candidly about the formal and informal deliberations and about the team's assessment of the other side's strategies and predicaments. The team, which spends countless hours with its interlocutors, can contribute to the modern peace process by sharing with the political leadership the situation, motives, and strategies of the other side, as well as the possible outcomes, gains, and compromises of the negotiation.

Naturally, each side tries to sell concessions at the highest price. It is thus important to leave the real concessions to the end. At the beginning of a negotiation, parties must put on the table a good draft that can become the basis of discussion. Good drafters know the value of words and should be present until the endgame. Political decision makers can best contribute to the process toward the end of negotiations, when most outstanding issues have been resolved. By recognizing their unique roles and responsibilities, peace leaders—both political leaders and negotiators—can leave negotiating to negotiators and ultimate decision making to those who hold that power.

A further critical tactical issue is the definition of the negotiation's deadline. The deadline operates most effectively if it is imposed by a third party, because intense negotiators tend to bluff about deadlines in order to force the other party to expose its most important concessions. Enforcement of a deadline is an excellent opportunity for the international community to support and encourage modern negotiations and thus to contribute to the cultivation of lasting peace between the two parties.

Reflection in the Media

Negotiators generally prefer to stay away from the media, and rightly so. However, avoidance of the press does not mean that negotiators should not play a role vis-à-vis the media or that the image of the negotiation is not important. The media is often used and misused by leaking information intended to influence the negotiation. The issues negotiators present to the media often emphasize the "red lines" or the concessions already received and boast about how staunchly the negotiators are defending the nation's cause.

Although such self-congratulatory campaigning is somewhat unavoidable, it is mostly futile and unhelpful. Instead, the reflection of negotiations in the media should be seen as an integral part of the peacemaking. It can be a mechanism by which to pass messages and transmit values in relation to common strategic goals, and to emphasize the advantage of compromise for the good of both sides.

The media also is a tool by which the public can learn about the new partner, its society, its problems, and its leaders. Humanization on the basis of equality is critical; the more equality can be brought into the hearts and minds of the constituencies, the more room the parties will have to maneuver.

The chief negotiators should issue very strict guidelines about dealing with the media in relation to the negotiations. My experience recommends that a very limited number of people can effectively liaise with the media about the negotiations, and maximum coordination between the two sides regarding the information presented will best contribute to creating lasting peace. Regular, joint communiqués about the negotiations should be succinct, encouraging the media to focus on stories that humanize the Other and that emphasize common strategic interests and the aim of reconciliation.

Media relations provide an occasion for each side to free itself from the unhelpful and untruthful monopoly on suffering, justice, and rights that each generally projects. To do so, the two sides can coordinate with their respective political superiors so that similar messages emanate from both sides of the table. They also can work together to speak to each other's media; it often is easier to sway public opinion with assurances from the former enemy that changes and benefits are on the way. Above all, the chief negotiators should be unforgiving toward those in the delegations who are indiscreet and fail to adhere to the guidelines the teams have set for themselves; transgressors should be relieved of their duties.

Joint strategizing between negotiators greatly increases the potential for success. It does not detract from the agonizing and manipulative battle of the core negotiation—after all, negotiations are intended to serve the interests of one's nation. But when the aim of the negotiation is a sustainable treaty—as it should be in a modern peace process—nurturing common interests is a vital endeavor.

Given that the sustainability of peace is dependent on its widespread societal support, negotiations must pave the way for balanced, positive effects. Even if one side is coming to the table following a "victory," it nonetheless is a grave mistake to take too much advantage of one's opponent. Such overkill in a negotiation will undoubtedly backfire in time. Negotiations will be most conducive to peace if they aim to create a balance of interests and motivation and are established within a framework of mutual respect and dignity. Negotiators must create an emotional and practical bridge to the future; relinquish hostility, excessive suspicion, and spite; and delve deeply to find empathy with the former enemy. Only in this way can negotiators forge a peace based on equality between former enemies.

When I saw Abu Ala on the other side of the table during the Oslo negotiations, I often felt I was looking in a mirror. This recognition was vital to our relationship as negotiators and as partners. People tend to focus on their own suffering and to forgive themselves more readily than they do their enemy. We remain suspicious of the Other, vacillating between hope and despair. In contrast, the discovery of another individual's identity engenders empathy—a recognition of commonality that must lie at the core of negotiations and peacemaking.

CHAPTER ELEVEN

The Peace Treaty

THE PEACE TREATY IS NOT AN END BUT A BEGINNING; IT IS the genesis of new relations between former enemies, a compass that guides cooperative and sustainable relationships. In line with the new peacemaking process, the peace treaty cannot merely concern itself with solutions to past tribulations, security arrangements, the distribution of spoils, and a formal definition of future relations. Historical peace treaties read like divorce papers, focused on the distribution of chattel with the aim of an amicable parting. The modern peace treaty should read more like the agreement of an arranged marriage—a relationship stemming not from idealism or love but from pragmatism, based on the realistic elements needed to sustain a relationship.

I have written about the need for a more transparent peace process. This is particularly true when it comes to the language of peace treaties. Not only do traditional agreements concentrate on subjects that have little to do with the real struggles of post-conflict societies, but also they often are littered with dense, legal jargon that may seem impenetrable to the average citizen. For example, the General Peace Agreement for Mozambique, Protocol II (1991) makes the following statement regarding the "criteria and arrangements for the formation and recognition of political parties":

> For the operation and full development of a multi-party democracy based on respect for and guarantees of basic rights and freedoms and based on pluralism of democratic political expression and organization under which

political power belongs exclusively to the people and is exercised in accordance with principles of representative and pluralistic democracy, the parties must have fundamentally democratic principles by which they must abide in practice and in their political activities.[1]

The principles in this part of the treaty—in essence, pluralism and democracy—are valuable, but the language of the statement is distancing and abstract. To make peace a truly participatory process, with the inclusion of all citizens as peacemakers, peace treaties should also be inviting and clearly written so that the concepts therein can be disseminated among as many people as possible.

Because the modern peace treaty is the foundation of modern peace, it is important for the agreement to consider and formalize within the document itself the four pillars of glocalization, peace ecology, peacebuilding, and creative diplomacy. Here, I describe a ten-part structure for modern peace agreements, outlining the conditions most conducive to a lasting peace. This structure can be tailored to the needs of each conflict situation and the demands of the parties involved, so that peace can be built within the specific cultural considerations of those societies.

Part 1: Goals and Vision

The introductory section serves as a reiteration of the treaty's commitment to modern peace. Here, peace leaders have the opportunity to state the treaty's goals as reconciliation and cooperation, not simply as the cessation of war. By formally recognizing the principles of mutual respect, equality, dignity, and respect for human rights and cultural and religious differences—potentially in conjunction with relevant UN covenants and declarations—the peace agreement can embody the values that are so fundamental to modern peace. The introduction is also a good place to offer a general, long-term vision of the future relationship between the signatories, with mention made of such issues as economic integration, confederative relations, joint territorial areas and more, depending on the circumstances.

Part 2: Definition of Peaceful Relations

The second part of the peace treaty can pave the way for future cooperation between the two parties by calling for the immediate establishment of diplomatic and consular relations, including embassies in the respective capitals (which can be helpful in the peacemaking process), without necessarily waiting for the full implementation of the treaty. Peaceful relations involve eradicating the impediments that existed during the conflict and replacing them with a comprehensive relationship in the economic, social, political, and cultural spheres. This section of the modern peace agreement can provide an important framework for lifting legal barriers that previously prevented cross-border cooperation. In other words, the representation of each country should not be restricted to formal diplomatic players but instead should welcome the participation of a broad coalition of peacemakers in various sectors.

Part 3: Regional Framework

Areas that have advanced systems for regional integration tend to be more stable and less likely to fall back into violence—the EU and ASEAN approaches are good examples. Peace is a strategic interest not only of the countries directly involved but also of those countries that are interdependent with the core conflict area. The third part of the modern peace treaty, therefore, acknowledges the importance of the region at large and offers ways to integrate the conflict area into the surrounding region. Neighboring countries then have the opportunity to lend their support to the agreement by committing to diplomatic, economic, and cultural ties with the conflict parties. Parliaments, councils of foreign ministers, and economic groups (both public and private) are all excellent channels for cooperation. This part of the treaty also can establish a financial mechanism—a regional peace fund or a development bank—to support peacebuilding projects by working with people and organizations within the core area on capacity-building and cooperative ventures.

Although these regional structures and activities generally become relevant only after the implementation of the conflict resolution, the location of the regional framework in the initial sections of the treaty indicates that regional peace is integral to peace within the core conflict area and that the region supports the peacemaking efforts.

Part 4: Rehabilitation

Economic and social rehabilitation of the conflict zone is imperative to the sustainability of peace. It is widely acknowledged, for example, that the decision to disband the Iraqi army in 2003 without conditions in place for the rehabilitation of those 250,000 soldiers was one of the major contributors to continued violence in Iraq.[2] A modern peace treaty must therefore be instrumental in ensuring that war economies—and the groups involved in their perpetuation—develop into fruitful peace economies linked by cooperative measures and ventures.

The treaty can outline means of eliminating potential legal and physical obstacles to cross-border economic links, and the measures each side must take to rehabilitate the conflict zone, particularly the repair and redevelopment of infrastructure and social support for those affected by conflict. Economic systems that function within the parameters of a free market economy can help spark economic growth. The economic institutions of each side need to be effective, transparent, and accountable; then, with the support of regional actors and the private sector, such institutions can provide local and foreign investors with the necessary incentives to give the conflict areas a much-needed economic boost.

The budgetary policy of each side should reflect a move toward a peace economy, decreasing defense budgets and increasing social, educational, and infrastructure budgets. Ideally, a budget forecast of this nature would appear in the treaty; however, critics might protest that peace treaties and internal politics should not intersect. In response, one could argue that although security arrangements and troop deployment are matters of internal decision making, such elements have always been legitimate in traditional peace treaties. There is no reason why budgetary policies cannot follow suit.

The rehabilitation of destroyed infrastructures and the creation of new cross-border links also will serve as a basis for important joint economic ventures—a feature that absolutely has a place in modern peace. Such ventures can be described in detail in the peace agreement, to illustrate their social and economic value for both sides, to lay the foundation for cooperative work, and to portray the benefits of peace to the respective constituencies.

Potentially more important than the physical rehabilitation of the conflict space is the rehabilitation of the populations. This endeavor, essential to any peace process, must assist those who have become underprivileged and scarred as a result of the conflict, including displaced citizens, refugees, the disabled, families in mourning, returning prisoners of war, and former soldiers—particularly child soldiers. For the sake of social justice, it is essential that the parties commit to investment in the weaker segments of society—those who might otherwise be the victims of peace. By ensuring that the distribution of peace dividends reaches those most in need, a peace agreement can help narrow socioeconomic gaps and thus increase regional stability.

Part 5: Peacebuilding

In neither theory nor practice do clear lines exist between economic recovery, peacebuilding, glocalization, and peace ecology; they are equally important and often overlap. However, rough delineations in this part of the treaty can help identify potential projects and areas of cooperation between the two parties. Economic recovery pertains to the economic measures executed by the parties, independently and jointly, in their move toward a peace economy.

Peacebuilding initiatives are most successful when they operate in tandem with diplomatic efforts. Whereas diplomatic regimes endeavor to solve issues of the past, peacebuilding practices are oriented toward the future. These practices, which enhance quality of life, can be quantified based on their multiplier effect and their capacity to save lives. From these points of view, cooperation on nutrition and health are extremely important.

Peacebuilding activities vary according to needs. These needs should be reflected in the modern peace treaty, with the fundamental need for peace exerting the strongest influence.

Part 6: Glocalization

Glocalization is a natural extension of peacebuilding. A modern peace treaty can provide a framework for specific measures to enhance city-to-city cooperation. By emphasizing interactivity in the treaty itself, peace leaders make the statement that glocalization is an integral requirement for a lasting peace.

It is important that this part of the agreement be detailed and extensive to ensure implementation and integration. For example, a peace treaty can establish committees, directed by mayors from each side of the conflict, to recruit local government workers for joint activities. A treaty also could support the creation of city triangles (one city from each side of the conflict and a third, international city), which would support development and municipal capacity building.

Peace leaders and peace bureaucrats can work together to identify ways of glocalizing peace in their unique regional context. Cooperative arrangements must be perceived as a core element of peacemaking, no less important than security. The decentralization of peace—participatory peace—is especially important during this era of rapid urbanization, to ensure that peace infiltrates all strata of society and is not merely saved for the elite.

Part 7: Peace Ecology

This section of the modern peace treaty allows both sides to commit to programs and activities designed to accelerate a revolution toward empathy and coexistence. For example, a joint campaign led by public relations professionals from both parties can market a new, common language of communication, emphasizing the benefits of peace and evoking a lasting feeling of trust and partnership between former enemies. Peace leaders also can use this section of the treaty to commit to presenting positive peace rhetoric and to making periodic appearances in the other side's media. This section goes to the core of negotiations, and a detailed outline of peace ecology activities—including peace education, cultural exchange, interfaith dialogue, and youth empowerment—will greatly improve the chances of successful implementation.

Part 8: Comprehensive Security

Although the security aspects in a modern peace treaty are less central than they were once considered, and in their traditional sense are insufficient on their own, they are still absolutely necessary. Security in the modern era, as it is manifested in a modern peace treaty, is achieved by diverse means. Both traditional and more innovative measures need to be employed to realize and sustain peace.

All sides previously engaged in the conflict must commit to a zero-tolerance rule regarding terror activity by dismantling terror infrastructures, including financing mechanisms, and taking on the responsibility of preventing all forms of terrorism. Cooperation between the parties and on a regional level will facilitate exchange of both intelligence and operational methods. Any violent activity taken on by antipeace elements must be utterly eradicated to cultivate an environment conducive to sustainable peace.

According to the tenets of modern peace, troop deployment on both sides of the border should be limited and must be defined in great detail in a modern peace treaty. Demilitarization along the conflict border will enhance trust and contribute to a positive peace ecology. Similarly, when border crossings are conducted in a way that respects the dignity of individuals and encourages cooperation, both parties will benefit from more effective and efficient security. Sea and air provisions can be dealt with according to international law and should resemble those of countries living within peaceful borders—thereby presenting a model for other security arrangements.

Cooperative security and monitoring measures, facilitated by joint security coordination centers, can support peace by building relationships between armies. A binational and multinational force can be established for the purposes of patrols, antiterror activities, and border protection. This type of joint security action—getting armies that have fought one another to start working together—provides practical value and, no less important, symbolic value.

International peacekeeping forces—involving binational or regional forces—can add great value by monitoring security arrangements and maintaining stability. International observers such as the United Nations or NATO also can provide crucial support and oversight for cross-border security cooperation. To ensure that peace is not merely a stage between wars and to limit the expansion of existing armies, detailed and transparent arms control agreements are an important component of the modern peace treaty. These clauses are related to the national priorities of each party, and specifically to the curtailment of defense budgets (as discussed in part 4 of the peace document).

These security arrangements will be most successful if they are independently effective while also being employed as peacebuilding measures that contribute to peace ecology through bilateral cooperation.

Part 9: Implementation Monitoring

Traditionally, monitoring the implementation of a peace agreement has centered on security and military aspects—but with the modern peace treaty's new concentration on the four pillars, this section of the document also widens its focus. Peace leaders can use this opportunity to define a comprehensive high-tech monitoring system that will supervise the implementation of all aspects of the treaty, including the goodwill and credibility of third parties (regional partners, major donors, and global actors).

Monitoring the implementation of the peace treaty is crucial to ensuring that all relevant parties are fulfilling their obligations and are contributing meaningfully to the process. Particularly during times of transition, measuring the development of peacebuilding projects and activities will help all parties and international actors identify which endeavors are most successful and which ones need more attention. Credible benchmark research—including tools such as the peace barometer or other survey methods undertaken by reliable international institutions—also can be used to continuously measure public attitudes toward peace, the former enemy, and the treaty implementation.

The triangular structure of city networking can be useful in monitoring regional peacebuilding, peace ecology, and glocalization of the treaty. Comprehensive reports regarding implementation, issued periodically by the relevant parties, can be useful as the focus of periodic summit meetings among the leaders. These meetings provide a forum for constructive dialogue, capacity building, and enhancement of the implementation of the treaty.

Part 10: International Involvement

Traditionally, the role of the international community in a peace treaty has focused on power and national interests: parties to the prior conflict seek political and economic support for transformations within their societies while third parties (from the international community) endeavor to obtain strategic footholds in the post-conflict region. This narrow-minded approach only perpetuates selfish aims instead of cultivating cooperation. A better strategy—one that can lead to regional growth as well as national transformation—is for international actors to model the behavior they want most to see in the post-conflict societies and to put structures into place to support the four pillars. By dedicating a section of the peace agreement to international contributions, all parties formalize the critical role of the international community in the core conflict area.

Although the international community certainly has a role in modern peacemaking, outside actors will be most effective if their contributions run parallel to a bilateral negotiation process, which remains the best approach to creating a modern treaty. The conflict parties play the key role in all aspects of peacemaking, and the role of the international community is to provide them with essential support during peacebuilding and treaty implementation.

The modern peace treaty is only one part of the peacemaking process—but it is a crucial one. By structuring this important document to emphasize the four pillars of modern peace as well as regional and international contributions, post-conflict parties can pave the way for all peacemaking activities that follow. A modern treaty that strives toward transparency and participation from many sectors of society can set up the framework for participatory implementation and cooperation.

CHAPTER 12

Implementation

PEACE PROCESSES HAVE TRADITIONALLY BEEN HIGHLIGHTED
by dramatic breakthroughs—those that lead to negotiations and
those that take place during negotiations. The other highlight is, of
course, the signing of the peace agreement. However, after these
highlights become vague memories, the road to peace becomes
arduous. Processes reach the critical point when they must be implemented. Even the best peace treaty, if only partially implemented,
will not result in the desired peace. Implementation is key.

Modernized peacemaking does not end when a modern treaty is
signed; those innovative approaches have a place in implementation
as well. The implementation process involves the legal framework
behind the movement from war to peace and the organizational
structure of governmental and nongovernmental bodies that will
deal with the implementation. Implementation occurs both internally (independently within each party) and jointly between both
parties.

I recognize that the implementation of a peace treaty happens
on many levels, and I make no claim to detail all of them here. It is
of course crucial that NGOs, businesses, civil society groups, and
international groups fulfill their duties as outlined in the agreement, and that they are held accountable.

However, in my experience, it is the governments of the two
post-conflict countries that have the opportunity and responsibility to provide a model for effective implementation. They, after all,
house the peace leaders and the many peace bureaucrats who have
represented their populations during negotiations, and who now
have the chance to open the implementation process to a wider

coalition of peacemakers. In this chapter, I present organizational recommendations, shaped by the four pillars of modern peace, that allow maximum coordination among government offices, NGOs, civil societies, and businesses.

It is not necessary for governments to build an entirely new framework in order to provide effective implementation; my recommendations here are based on basic organizational structures that most governments already share: a prime minister or president (what I refer to here as the executive office), the office that deals with foreign affairs (the foreign ministry), offices that deal with financial affairs (the economic ministries), the office that deals with matters of security and defense (the defense ministry), and the justice ministry. Although this chapter becomes fairly technical, it's important for citizens to understand the ins and outs of implementation. Governments are created to serve the needs of their people, and how better to do that than by establishing committees and councils focused primarily on implementing and facilitating peace?

I also recognize that in some countries—particularly those that have experienced long periods of conflict—corruption can have a severe impact on the effectiveness of government programs and the amount of relief that reaches the people. Corruption is a challenge not easily surmounted; fighting graft is something that must happen on national and international levels, with the support and guidance of the World Bank, the IMF, the United Nations, and other international organizations. A corrupt government can seriously limit the potential of large-scale peacebuilding programs and reforms, but this does not mean that peacebuilding should be ignored in the meantime.

I believe one of the strengths of the organizational structure I recommend here is that it places peacebuilding power in the hands of many, including representatives from government ministries as well as actors from the private sector, the NGO community, and civil societies. By balancing the responsibilities of peacebuilding among a wide range of actors, the chances of successful implementation improve dramatically and a few rotten apples are far less likely to spoil peacemaking as a whole. This comprehensive approach reflects the fundamental nature of a decentralized peace process: the momentum toward peace can be so great that the occasional obstacle is simply swept aside.

Internal Implementation

The initial step of domestic implementation of the peace treaty is legislative in nature. Laws that forbid contact or cooperation with the enemy only perpetuate a culture of war. To move toward a culture of peace, governments can abolish all such laws. It is also wise to legislate in favor of the peace treaty.

A **ministerial steering committee** can be established at the outset as a channel for relevant ministers in the implementation process. Chaired by the head of the executive office and made up of the ministers of foreign affairs, finance, defense, and justice, the ministerial steering committee can solidify efforts to ensure that all government branches are fulfilling their responsibilities as outlined in the peace treaty. The crucial aspect is that the peace process, particularly its implementation, is being guided and supported by the elected leaders of the country.

To oversee the day-to-day work of implementation, an inter-ministerial working group, the **national peace council** (parallel to existing national security councils), can be established. This working group essentially represents the senior officials of the ministries working in the steering committee. Through the national peace council, these peace leaders can be in regular contact with various key players, to develop improved approaches to implementation and to respond to any unforeseen events or setbacks. The various ministers and senior officials represented in the steering committee and the national peace council have the opportunity to reform relevant structures by integrating some of their functions. In countries where the composition of the government has been dislocated, institutions that deal with rehabilitation and peacebuilding issues will need to be rebuilt or constructed from scratch; the national peace council can be instrumental in helping this reconstruction.

All other committees and groups can work under the steering committee and the national peace council, but they would originate in and be staffed by different ministries. Here, I will outline in greater detail the structural changes in each government ministry that will favor effective implementation.

The Executive Office (Prime Minister/President)

The executive office possesses ultimate responsibility for the whole process and therefore has the responsibility to ensure that implementation rests on the four pillars of modern peace. Having access to all personnel, tools, and information can help the executive office become more efficient and effective. The executive office can define the agenda of the steering committee by gaining information from all relevant reports flowing from the national peace council, the negotiation teams, the intelligence services, the government ministries, the heads of local governments, the NGOs, and the international system. The national leader has the duty to encourage a culture of meticulous implementation of the agreement by both parties, according to timelines, and to ensure that the commitment to implementation penetrates all operational levels.

The executive office can embody the values of participatory peace and peace ecology. It also can support implementation by remaining in constant contact with the various government ministries and by appointing various teams to deal with communication with the other side. Regular and open contact between domestic ministries and those of the new peace partner can help build interdependent and cooperative relationships, which will lead to more effective implementation. "Peace units" established by the executive office within each ministry also can be used to monitor the work and report to the ministry's guiding authority. Although the foreign ministry plays a central role in coordinating relations with other countries, it is important for the head of the executive office to remain personally involved in ensuring that international partners remain a part of the implementation process.

The Foreign Ministry (or State Department)

In many countries, the defense ministry takes a leading role in the peacemaking effort, but this could serve in some ways as a continuation of the war effort. Peace is fundamentally a civilian concept, even if it includes security-related components. As relations between former enemies normalize, peace relations will slowly drift toward the realm of foreign affairs and diplomacy. From this perspective, the foreign ministry is in a position not only to acquire more political clout but also to procure the expertise that will allow it to coordinate much of the implementation of a peace treaty, including political and security issues, regional economics and trade, infrastructure, peacebuilding, and peace ecology. Foreign affairs and cooperation between former enemies are crucial components of cultivating a lasting modern peace, which is why the foreign ministry can be so intimately involved in implementation.

Cultural exchange and tolerance are also imperative to the work of the foreign ministry because a switch in attitudes about the former enemy is required. The notion of "enemy" must gradually be relinquished and the idea of "neighbor" must be permitted to surface. An open mind about a foreign culture is far more important than expertise in the history of the new partner, because much of a nation's perception of history was formed during the conflict. In the same vein, the foreign ministry should encourage peace officials to learn the spoken language of the former enemy, to bolster the creation of a common language.

As a whole, the foreign ministry can be structured to perform three core functions in the implementation of the modern peace treaty:

1. general coordination of implementation;

2. formalization of cross-border relationships; and

3. recruitment of other governmental bodies and NGOs to participate in implementation.

Through these three functions, the foreign ministry will maximize its opportunities to align implementation with the four pillars of modern peace.

1. **General coordination of implementation.** The foreign ministry can coordinate implementation of the peace process by government officials, based on the directives of the national peace council. Much of the foreign ministry's implementation work deals with the thousands of technical details required to solve the modernized peace puzzle. For this purpose, the foreign ministry can establish a **government peace coordination unit** to work in conjunction with the peace units in the relevant ministries. The foreign ministry's unit can request from the national peace council the resources required to fulfill peace functions and harmonize the implementation work.

During implementation, parties are generally less forgiving of their counterpart's imperfections than of their own. However, tolerance of such shortcomings should not show a bias; impatience with flaws in implementation is required for both parties to the agreement. Mutual understandings that lead to certain flexibilities and changes during implementation are unavoidable, but these should be kept to a minimum so as to avoid straying from the strategic path of modern peace.

Frequently, both the laborious implementation and the change in mind-set required to work with the peace partner demand a fresh approach and specialized skills. To this end, the foreign ministry would benefit greatly from the establishment of a training program for officials within and outside the ministry, to enhance existing capacities and to develop the new ones necessary for peacemaking. Instructors with senior peacemaking experience can contribute a vast depth of knowledge and experience to capacity-building programs.

2. **Formalization of cross-border relationships.** Essentially, the foreign ministry is responsible for formalizing the relationship with the peace partner, including establishing formal, diplomatic, consular, and commercial relationships and appointments. It is imperative that the diplomats tasked with launching the delegation in the capital of the former enemy be proficient, with firsthand experience of the peace process. These diplomats—much like peace leaders and negotiators during earlier stages in the peace process—must be effective, open-minded communicators who can be easily understood and who will report to their leaders with candor. Moreover, as representatives of their country, they must endeavor to reflect the positive characteristics of their country—including modesty, dignity, and curiosity—and to express the culture of their country.

In further formalizing new peace relationships for the future, the foreign ministry can locate commonly ratified international covenants, agreements, and treaties and determine their relevance regarding issues such as trade relations, the environment, and drug trafficking. In the same context, if the treaty stipulates any sort of federal relations, the foreign ministry is in the best position to be responsible for the practical coordination of those relations.

3. **Recruitment of other governmental bodies and NGOs to participate in implementation.** In conjunction with the economic ministries, the foreign ministry can establish a **committee for regional development** and should play a leading role in this committee. In this context, post-conflict societies can look to existing regionally integrated systems, such as the European Union and ASEAN, as good models that can be tailored to their specific regional situation. Through the minister and senior officials, the ministry can participate in regional institutions within both the political and the economic spheres—for example, a regional financial mechanism in which national bank and finance ministry representatives participate. For such contributions to be made effectively, and to fulfill the economics-related clauses of the peace treaty, the foreign ministry must acquire more economic expertise.

To create peace, relationships between former enemies must

ultimately be shifted into the realm of international relations; the foreign ministry is thus best situated to be in the driver's seat. For the purpose of coordinating the governmental and nongovernmental peacebuilding activities emphasized in the treaty, the foreign ministry can establish a **peacebuilding committee** headed by an individual with project implementation experience. The committee's members would include officials from relevant governmental ministries, such as finance, education, culture, sport, and youth. This committee can encourage a more participatory peace by inviting representatives from the main NGOs and private-sector organizations that wish to and are able to contribute to the peacebuilding process.

The peacebuilding committee is an opportunity to serve the needs of both parties by uniting these needs with the stipulations of the peace treaty. The committee can provide the impetus for the triangular project work to be undertaken by the parties to the agreement and the international community. The committee's projects will be most effective with the advent of local, regional expertise, because outside expertise is expensive and over time will abandon the region for other interests.

The foreign ministries of both parties also can emphasize equality throughout the implementation stage; if an economic gap surfaces during implementation, for instance, the peacebuilding project implementation team can try to maintain a positive peace ecology by narrowing the gap without patronizing the weaker side. However, both parties are naturally equipped with different capabilities and thus can benefit from equal exchange of knowledge, capacities, and skills.

The implementation process will have the greatest chance of success if it is based in the peace treaty but also is flexible. Although it is important to plan and execute all clauses of the treaty, some room should be left for new initiatives in the spheres of peacebuilding, glocalization, and peace ecology. The government can be particularly flexible with NGOs because the NGO community has a great capacity for creative peace and development projects.

Spontaneity is the soul of the NGO world, and their cooperation with the government should not place them in a bureaucratic straitjacket. NGOs represent a crucial arm of peace bureaucrats, and their "higher good" mandates make them potential ambassadors for each side. The foreign ministry can recognize the importance of NGOs by introducing local NGOs to the other side and by appointing informal ambassadors from academia, NGOs, and social institutions to work with the other side.

The glocalization of peace according to the treaty requires a transfer of peacemaking power and resources from the national governmental level to the local level. A **committee for decentralized peace** can tackle this transfer in tandem with a coalition of representatives from the foreign ministry, the executive office, and a **council of local government**. The council of local government, comprising mayors from both sides of the conflict and from a third, international city, can provide much-needed contact between citizens and government, through the channel of city leaders. In accordance with the treaty, the peace city triangle can concentrate on peacebuilding through joint activities focused on capacity building, urban topics, youth, and the creation of links between civil societies. City diplomacy during implementation can create the participatory peace required for the sustainability of the peace effort. In this context, the government must learn to loosen its grip on power.

In the past, issues of peace ecology have been taken for granted during the implementation of a treaty, but they do not take care of themselves. A **committee for peace ecology,** established by the foreign ministry and the executive office, can provide the framework to ensure that the values of human rights, equality, and cooperation are infused into society. Although the foreign ministry does not usually deal with issues relating to national public opinion, in this instance they have the ultimate aim of working alongside their counterparts in the foreign ministry of the other side to positively influence public opinion in both populations. To truly reflect peace values, the public relations attitude of the foreign ministry must change from merely justifying national positions to proving the merits of cooperative peace. A communication bridge between the committee for peace ecology and the national peace council can affect one of the most important elements of the peace mood—the rhetoric of the leadership.

Peace ecology, like the other pillars, can only be fully realized when it invites the participation of all members of society. To make the move toward peace ecology more inclusive, the government's committee for peace ecology can create several subcommittees that rely on the involvement of outside groups to cultivate an atmosphere of peace.

First, a **subcommittee for public opinion campaigns,** comprising government officials and private-sector operators, can use research on public attitudes to plan and execute an aggressive campaign to "sell" peace and the peace treaty to society and to legitimize partnership with the other side. Research that provides insight into changing attitudes about the former enemy and new partner (a peace barometer) will be highly useful. Local and international private-sector companies participating in the venture should be selected according to governmental tenders—not everyone who can sell Coca-Cola can sell peace. The public relations professionals not only must be passionate about peace but also must be open-minded so that they can realize the possibilities of peace during the transition period. Integrating different kinds of expertise and professional background is very effective for the implementation of the modern peace treaty.

Second, a **subcommittee for media relations** can be created to sell peace to the media, the key channel for transferring messages and peace campaigns to the public. Traditionally, journalists have emphasized the negative stereotypes of the other side, sensationalized setbacks in the peace process, and avoided coverage of the human side of reconciliation. It is, of course, unthinkable to recruit the media into a pro-peace position; a one-sided approach, even when it promotes peace, is nothing more than propaganda. However, the media can become the means to portray a balanced image of the process and of the other party, thereby broadening the perspective of members of the public. Influential journalists from both sides of the border can be encouraged to work together to explore the plight of the former enemy.

The third and final subcommittee under the committee for peace ecology can involve cultural leaders in a **subcommittee for intercultural relations**. Surprisingly, experience has proven that artists —the most cosmopolitan and avant-garde sector of society—seldom step outside their own environment to spontaneously cooperate with the other side. According to the peace treaty, however, efforts must be directed toward cultural exchange, including joint artistic endeavors. Through this subcommittee, two distinctive cultures can create a milieu for multiculturalism during peacetime.

As in all implementation work, initial responsibility for monitoring is best assumed independently by the foreign ministry and other relevant government actors, informed by nongovernmental information and reports; later, the work can be done in conjunction with the peace partner. Monitoring is imperative to successful realization of the modern peace treaty, and those responsible for monitoring should be extremely sensitive to the flaws that will surface during implementation. Micromanagement can be useful under these circumstances.

Because our modern peace centers on cooperation beyond national boundaries, it falls to the foreign ministry to administer all implementation efforts that involve the international community, even if such activity is beyond the scope of foreign affairs. For example, the foreign ministry can assist the defense ministry on issues such as peacekeeping forces, international security pacts, and politico-military security pacts, because those issues (in a modern peace) necessarily involve outside parties and cooperation.

To best fulfill its implementation functions, the concept of a modern foreign ministry would greatly benefit from serious reform. The traditional foreign ministry tends to be a propaganda machine for a nation's positions and actions during conflict. During peacetime, however, it should abandon its narrow, nationalistic views and promote the tenets of modern peace by becoming a peace ministry, progressing from a ministry of rhetoric to a ministry of action—less protocol, more projects. Such reforms can grant the foreign ministry more political clout around the governmental table and in the country than it has during periods of conflict, when an inferiority complex weakens the foreign ministry in relation to the defense establishment. In a modern peace, the foreign ministry must represent the national interest by bringing peace and prosperity; diplomats must become soldiers for peace.

Reform in the foreign ministry is also needed on a practical level. As regional political and economic developments ascend the political agenda, capable diplomats will be the best representatives of modern peace values. Successful peacemaking is measurable and reflects the skills of the diplomats in action—a proposition at which not all diplomats will rejoice. Training and supervision will help diplomats take full advantage of economic opportunities that arise, such as international investment or political opportunities in the multilateral diplomatic world that may produce resources for projects. Under the terms of a modern peace treaty, project development and implementation is not a responsibility traditionally associated with diplomacy, so expert input will be particularly beneficial. In addition, comprehensive security reforms must be applied; a politico-military unit should be established by the foreign ministry, working closely with the defense ministry.

These recommendations are difficult, but they are necessary to make the implementation process both inclusive and effective in cultivating lasting peace on a national and international scale. One way to support the reform process is to recruit a relatively large number of young diplomats with the appropriate qualifications, drive, and openness to change. Youth diplomats not only will encourage systemic reform but also will persuade the old guard of ambassadors to become more reform minded. In 1995, while I was director general of the Israeli Foreign Ministry, we convened an international conference called Reforms of the Modern Foreign Service Universally. This conference was held soon after the similar comprehensive reform I was leading in the foreign ministry. It has been long obvious that such reform is needed, but it is even more desirable when implementing modern peace.

Economic Ministries

If a country's economic ministries (those dealing with finance, trade, and industry) are to successfully contribute to the peace-building initiatives of a modern peace treaty, they also would benefit from some degree of reform. Economic ministry officials can pave the way for joint ventures by coming up with ways to build financial, project, and trade bridges to the new peace partner and to international partners, as well as by reprioritizing the budget in terms of the new peace economy and the implementation of the peace treaty. To ensure openness in cross-border relationships, this budget should be completely transparent and accountable to the peace partner and to the international community.

The peace unit in the ministry of finance is in a good position to work simultaneously on the implementation of the treaty and on an economic road map that advances the national economy into the new peace era, dispersing peace dividends between the new partners to close the socioeconomic gap. The ministry of finance can coordinate details with all relevant government ministries and can espouse the ideals of participatory peace by including the private sector in its proposals and activities.

In cases where the national economies have been devastated by war, the ministry of finance can support rehabilitation and growth by building solid, modern, reliable, and transparent economic institutions, including sector-oriented economic ministries, investment agencies, infrastructure units, and social services. The ministry of finance and the international community can work closely on the provision and utilization of peace aid, including rehabilitation assistance, infrastructure development, peacebuilding projects, decentralized cooperation, peace ecology, institution building, and so on.

The modern peace treaty is the basis for cooperative and integrative approaches involving the peace partners, the international community, and the private sector. Implementation by the economic ministries can therefore be centered on the facilitation of the conditions necessary for economic cooperation with the new partner and the international community. Under the auspices of the modern peace treaty, the economic ministries can support joint ventures in the areas of rehabilitation, infrastructure development, free movement of people and goods, food security, peri-urban development, development of specialized trade zones, tourism, and more. The ministry of finance has an excellent opportunity to display uncharacteristic generosity by cooperating with the peace partner, even while maintaining a rigid fiscal policy. Such a show of mutual trust and cooperation would represent a symbolic move toward peace ecology and coexistence.

Defense Ministry

Just as other ministries can change the way they approach peace-making, the ministry of defense can become a role model for the transition from a mind-set of war to a mind-set of peace. During wartime, the ministry of defense and the army take the reins regarding decision making, and the necessary transition toward a more modest role during peacetime is not simple. However, the role and authority assumed by the ministry of defense during conflict can be renounced, respectfully, allowing the diplomatic and economic sectors to contribute to the security sector. After all, peace is the ultimate line of defense. As outlined in the modern peace treaty, special units can be created to coordinate redeployment and to handle relations with international peacekeepers. The ministry of defense also can be responsible for land areas, sea areas, and airspace according to maps and terms set forth in the modern peace treaty.

With the success of the modern peace, the defense establishment will inevitably shrink. There will be a reduction in the number of army personnel and a transformation of military industries into civilian industries. To implement such changes in a politico-military way and develop a comprehensive and integrative concept of security, the ministry of defense can establish a **committee for security issues and relations** made up of members of the army, intelligence personnel, and foreign and finance ministry officials. This committee, with particular emphasis on the foreign ministry element, also can be responsible for the coordination of international peacekeepers. As security becomes a joint venture rather than the sole responsibility of the defense establishment, such cooperation might be difficult for the ministry of defense to absorb, but cooperation is essential for maintaining stability and trust between the parties.

The modern peace treaty entails radical changes in terms of cooperative operations with the former enemy in the security domain, particularly with respect to combating terrorism. Having previously faced each another on the battlefield, it is no easy task to begin to exchange intelligence information, to halt terrorism financing, to jointly and actively prevent hostile activity, and to halt nonconventional proliferation. The parties can demonstrate their commitment to peace by becoming members of the Nuclear Non-Proliferation Treaty alliance, assuming there are no other nuclear parties engaging them. Furthermore, cooperation along the border and at border crossings is crucial to a peaceful environment, because border crossings represent direct interactions between citizens of both sides.

Modern warfare is deteriorating, and the greatest danger lies in the proliferation of nonconventional weapons. Not only can the parties work together to combat this threat, but they can also work with their regional and international partners, using a spectrum of tools ranging from boycotts to collective force, to reduce support for countries and constituencies that sustain terrorism.

Joint Implementation

Although each party has a responsibility to work independently, systematically, and scrupulously toward implementation of the modern peace treaty, the cooperative nature of modern peace emphasizes joint implementation. The purpose of joint work is to ensure transparency and flexibility in the implementation process, to rectify flaws as needed along the way, and to cooperatively labor on all peacebuilding elements. It also engenders a joint sense of responsibility and helps avoid public finger-pointing about the other side's implementation method, or lack thereof, which would pollute the vital peace ecology.

To effectively implement the treaty, the existing implementation units on both sides of the conflict border can work together in joint committees, according to the structure of the peace treaty. A timeline for implementation can be ascertained by the committees to ensure a constant dynamic between developing the peace and implementing the agreement.

Joint Steering Committee

The existing steering committees of the parties can create an overarching body to oversee the implementation process, to deal with issues that surface, and to decide on possible additions or changes to the agreement. This committee can be cochaired by the two heads of the executive offices (who should periodically hold joint summits), with the foreign ministers as deputies.

Joint Peace Council

The parties' existing peace councils can come together to deal with day-to-day monitoring of implementation according to a systematic matrix. They would report to the joint steering committee. This council also can provide a forum for the exchange of information about shifts in each side's political and social agenda, to enhance mutual understanding. The parties can use this joint framework to assist each other in their respective peace training programs. The negotiating teams must remain assembled for the purpose of negotiating any issues, such as additions or amendments, that may surface.

Joint Committee for Formal Relations

This committee can deal with diplomatic representation on both sides as well as all activities relating to the normalization of formal relations as outlined in the treaty.

Joint Committee for Economic Relations

This committee can deal with all joint economic aspects of the treaty, the economic peace relations such as trade zones, trade arrangements, infrastructure links, food security, technological development, joint projects, and so on. Peace process and peace economy budget specifications can be made available to both sides to ensure transparency.

Joint Committee for Regional Development

This committee can work to ensure that the regional framework stipulated by the modern peace agreement will be executed. By strategizing together with respect to regional cooperation and the peace process, the parties can approach their potential regional partners.

Joint Committee for Peacebuilding

Following the preparatory work of each independent peacebuilding committee, this joint committee is responsible for the implementation of peacebuilding projects according to the peace treaty. The committee can comprise members of the two national committees, the foreign ministries, and various local NGOs. The work on the ground can be done by appropriate experts and professionals, to maximize effectiveness. The committee can open its efforts to a wider coalition of peacemakers by involving the participation of relevant players from the international community, donor organizations, and NGOs. Implementing sound peacebuilding projects generally translates into the creation of a continual or even a multiplicative process. The committee can promote such a process, activate and monitor it, and attempt to locate financing from public and private sources.

Joint Committee for a Decentralized Peace (Glocalization)

The structure of this committee can be predetermined by the necessary preparatory work assigned to both sides. The committee can create a triangular framework of cities while members of the two foreign ministries develop a strategic direction for the triangular networks. These peace city triangles can implement the treaty by enlisting mayors, municipal officials, and local civil society units to participate in a variety of cooperative projects. These triangles are dynamic and can boost cooperative opportunities within and beyond their association. It is thus integral that this implementation structure be sustained and ambitiously expanded with time.

Joint Committee for Peace Ecology

The national, three-tier structure of the committee for peace ecology can be emulated for this joint committee, which would comprise foreign ministry personnel and major actors from each subcommittee—public relations, media, and culture. The subcommittees can implement the campaigns outlined in the modern peace treaty and can intensify the public relations, media, and cultural exchange campaigns initiated by each of the national subcommittees. The objective is to engage a broad range of social strata in cultural ties that enhance mutual understanding and respect.

Joint Security Committee

Experience has shown that, paradoxically, former security personnel are capable of rapidly creating a common language, despite their previous skirmishes. The implementation process undertaken by the joint security committee can be grounded in this common language—simultaneously emphasizing, however, that peace does not emanate from traditional modes of security. It is important to fastidiously implement the security-related clauses of the treaty, particularly those related to deployment and demilitarization, and flexibility among members is crucial to the establishment of joint working habits, particularly during times of potential crisis.

In the event that the peace process becomes stalled midway, violence will almost inevitably break out. The joint security committee can therefore establish three subcommittees that focus specifically on ways to maintain the peace. The first group can be a **joint subcommittee for the fight against terrorism.** Because terrorism—even nonconventional terrorism—is most likely the means that would be employed to jeopardize peace, this framework can be both bilateral and multilateral, bringing regional and international players onto the scene. The second group can be a **joint subcommittee for peacekeeping,** which also can be both bilateral and multilateral, to implement the peacekeeping clauses of the peace treaty and to enhance ongoing security dialogue. A third subcommittee, the **joint subcommittee for arms control,** can work toward the nonproliferation of conventional and nonconventional weapons.

Joint Committee for Youth-Related Issues

This committee can be the only unit that operates independently of the peace treaty. Because modern peace extends beyond the present horizon, youth must be involved at all levels: implementing youth-related issues, changing social attitudes toward peace and the Other, and building the foundations for a future peace leadership.

Joint Trilateral Committees

Because international community involvement is integral to the peace process, possible joint committees involving the parties to the agreement can be established, including the parties to an agreement with the United States, the parties to an agreement with the European Union and others, or even parties to an agreement with a single country such as Japan. The involvement of third parties is important in the postnegotiation stage because the experience and resources of the international community are essential even after the conflict has been resolved.

Ultimately, the successful implementation of a peace treaty is not just about the line-by-line fulfillment of the agreement's provisions. Implementation relies on flexible and creative cooperation between governments, NGOs, businesses, and civil societies, and may require those bodies to adapt to new developments during the process. Implementation is not a one-time endeavor. Rather, it requires years of commitment to upholding the peace agreement and to ensuring that the principles of human rights and equality become sewn into the very fabric of post-conflict societies.

CHAPTER 13

International Roles and Reforms

PEACE CANNOT HAPPEN IN A VACUUM; REGIONAL PARTNERS to the conflict societies, and the international community at large, can provide critical support and encouragement throughout the modern peacemaking process. The transition toward comprehensive peace and development aid requires a different approach to rules and regulations on the part of the international community, including the United Nations, the World Bank, the IMF, and individual countries, beginning with members of the Group of Eight (G-8).

Peace is a necessary component of the development of post-conflict countries, a truth that the international community can recognize through solid financial support. Peace aid not only can provide an impetus toward economic growth but also can foster the creation of economic relations that will lead to the successful implementation of the peace treaty.

The international community can greatly improve the quantity and quality of assistance provided for the rehabilitation and development of former war economies and for the cooperative measures to be undertaken by the post-conflict parties. If a substantial portion—15 percent or more—of total governmental assistance to conflict resolution were earmarked for cooperative projects, post-conflict societies would be formally supported in their joint peacebuilding efforts. The international community currently supports post-conflict areas according to the rules and regulations of developmental aid, but international aid can hardly be interpreted as a successful endeavor. When peace assistance goes hand in hand with development, peacebuilding is no longer a side note but a priority.

The isolation that develops as a result of conflict means that conflict zones often lack experience in regional development. The international community has the opportunity to guide the post-conflict area toward regional economic integration and interdependence. This integration covers areas such as legal matters, infrastructure links, investment policies, financial mechanisms (e.g., funds and guarantees), project development, and political cooperation. Such integration may well pay peace dividends on the economic front, but it also could spill over into the spheres of culture, education, youth, and so on.

The most recent and successful example of the integration phenomenon is the European Union, which is considered an extraordinary achievement. However, Europeans are reluctant to guide other regions toward a similar structure, claiming that others are not yet ripe for integration. Europeans prefer to compete with the United States for the dominant diplomatic and strategic role in the different regions, giving the impression that what is good for Europe is not good for others but that what is right for the United States is right for Europe.

Unfortunately for Brussels, both assumptions are wrong on a global scale: different regions in the world certainly can learn from the European experience, and Europe currently cannot compete with the United States in clout and influence. The European structure comprises the essence of modern-day diplomacy, and by guiding other regions toward similar regional frameworks, the European Union improves its chances of achieving influence and political clout in the future.

Therefore, the European Union, in cooperation with the United States and the World Bank, can contribute to modern peacemaking by supporting efforts toward integrative regional economic investment. The political leadership of the European Union can take on a leadership role in this context, as can nongovernmental players and the private sector, whose experience in efficient economic and regional development is invaluable.

Peacebuilding, Glocalization, and Peace Ecology

By definition, peacebuilding is a less organized and more spontaneous process than other aspects of peacemaking, because it originates in all sorts of arenas and because it involves nongovernmental organizations. If the security aspects of peacemaking are the most systematic, the peacebuilding aspects are the most anarchic; intensive, hand-in-hand peacebuilding activities create a critical mass of momentum that contributes to peacemaking.

The role of the international community in the sphere of peacebuilding is essentially to provide legitimacy to the peacebuilding efforts. Significant financing can be channeled to peacebuilding activities in the core post-conflict area; those activities will be most effective if the roles of international and local NGOs are reconciled for maximum coverage.

NGOs can help create the orchestrated anarchy in which they operate. International NGOs with experience in conflict regions can create the right atmosphere for peacebuilding by lending their proficiency, passion, and commitment to peace and humanitarian values. Governments and foundations can lend their support through fiscal and legal measures, giving NGOs the flexibility to operate as necessary in sensitive areas. Private-sector companies also have an important role to play in peacebuilding activities, often inspired and guaranteed by the governments of their countries. Such companies can best aid the peacebuilding process by ensuring that activities are more effective, efficient, and even potentially profitable, generating greater peace dividends.

As previously outlined, decentralization and city-to-city diplomacy are very useful for the purposes of peace and development, but their potential remains untapped. Although the concept of twin cities is not new, it generally represents little more than protocol and folklore. In our decentralized peace, however, cities can assume quasi-state functions in relation to peacebuilding.

The international community can contribute to modern peace in this context by rousing and empowering wealthy, developed, and peaceful cities to work with cities across divides in post-conflict areas. Such empowerment involves financing, brainpower, know-how, and encouragement on neutral territory, encouraging joint activities and dialogue. A good portion of aid money—up to 10 percent—can be channeled through local governments to minimize administrative costs and maximize the amount of assistance that reaches the needy.

The third, or mediating, cities serve to facilitate joint activities and dialogue between post-conflict cities by providing a neutral meeting point and by offering the knowledge and assets to aid peacebuilding activities. The third city also can provide important capacities for urban areas (on both sides, or on only one side) and can recruit the goodwill of its civil society to operate in tandem with local civil society organizations from the post-conflict region.

There are many examples of third-city contributions that illustrate the success of the glocalization theory, including Barcelona, Spain–Nablus–Rishon Le-Zion (youth dialogue); Rome-Kigali (exchange of agricultural expertise); Baltimore-Freetown (provision of additional garbage trucks for the Sierra Leone capital); Washington, DC–Addis Ababa; and Seattle, Washington–Haiphong, Vietnam. The international community should encourage these cities to continue their peacebuilding activities and should inspire more third cities to participate in the process. It should recruit for that purpose the aid of international organizations such as the World Bank; the Glocal Forum; UN-Habitat, the UN instrument responsible for city operations; and United Cities and Local Governments, a global NGO that operates on the local government level in hundreds of cities.

Peace ecology is another important element that the international community can foster. Marketing peace to civilians and constituencies has seldom been perceived by the international community as an important element of peacemaking. In regions where peace prevails, peace is generally taken for granted, as is the perception that most people reject war and support peace. But this is not the case.

In conflict zones, many constituencies have developed negative stereotypes of the enemy; there is a kind of comfort in the familiar status quo of conflict and hostility.

The international community can help conflict parties create an environment of peace and can influence the conflict-laden values dominant in such societies. World leaders can demonstrate the importance of peace ecology through rhetoric that reflects peaceful values. Most Western nations have cultural and information-dissemination institutions, such as the British Council, that work with counterpart institutions in conflict countries to generate peace-promoting public relations campaigns. It is important to encourage multiculturalism in post-conflict environments by holding pluralistic events that promote respect and tolerance; such values almost always fall victim to conflict.

Public relations events and campaigns also can be instituted by the international public sector, working with their counterparts from the post-conflict region. A public relations campaign event can intelligently and aggressively contextualize each region in terms of culture and environment and can advance peaceful coexistence. In the same vein, the international community can galvanize its academic institutions to work with peers in conflict areas to create an academic literature that endorses tolerance and negates the stereotypes encouraged by such literature during the conflict years. The most successful modern peace agreements introduce tangible goods and peace dividends into the conflict region and influence those community members who fail to recognize the value of peace.

Security Arrangements

International contributions to security in post-conflict areas can strengthen local forces and provide additional support for cooperative military activities. The security functions of the international community include assistance in antiterror activity through intelligence, monitoring of the peace treaty and all control agreements, and peacekeeping in border areas. This kind of aid can be acquired primarily from the United States and the European Union, but possibly also from regional players.

International peacekeepers also can take on a peacebuilding function; they can secure locations for joint ventures in engineering and employee training in various industries, in addition to providing assistance with prefeasibility studies. The most useful characteristics of UN and other international peacekeepers thus include both peacekeeping and peacebuilding skills.

A further security role for the international community lies in assisting post-conflict countries in their demilitarization process, including the transformation of military industries into civilian ones and the retraining of military personnel for civilian life. These demilitarization activities are important components of the social and economic rehabilitation process of post-conflict areas; the move also is symbolic of the transition from war to peace.

An important aspect of the relationship between the international community and post-conflict countries lies in the pacts between them that guarantee national security—or, preferably, regional security. A post-conflict country may have created a security pact or an agreement for antiterror training and intelligence exchange with a particular country, region, or international institution; however, the most effective collaborations add to regional stability and political security rather than detracting from it. These arrangements can exist, for example, between a former conflict country or region and NATO, as exemplified by the Partnership for Peace, a pact between NATO and former Eastern Bloc countries. This partnership has stabilized the region by demanding both security cooperation and political coordination, and it has linked Eastern Europe with a stable system of governance. Such a model could be used as the basis for partnerships to enhance cooperation and stability in other regions.

In a peace setting, security arrangements that run parallel to political arrangements will be most effective; political will and cooperation will create the common interests that sustain security and uphold stability, rather than security creating common interests. The United States, given its military capacity and willingness to use it, can take the lead on this approach by making use of its unmatched ability to plan and implement in a strategic fashion.

By looking at the role of the international community in its entirety we can create a multisector approach, employing a diversity of players led by the US administration, in areas such as economic recovery, regional development, peacebuilding, decentralization, and comprehensive security. Support will be most effective coming from governments, multilateral organizations, NGOs, private-sector groups, and social and cultural institutions as well as from the United Nations, the United States, the European Union, Japan, the World Bank, the IMF, and other relevant regional players.

The international community is a key part of this complex puzzle and must maintain its clear orientation toward creating and sustaining peace. Peacemaking is about mixing apples and oranges, and it requires an interdisciplinary approach to the content and the actors.

International Reforms

The international community cannot execute its functions in the modern peace process without large-scale reforms. The repeated threats of the use of nonconventional weapons, in addition to the failure of current security and peace doctrines, may result in the collapse of international stability. Consequently, a change in the international attitude about the implementation of modern peace is both probable and necessary. A revolutionary approach has the potential to increase the effectiveness and efficiency of international actors. Peace on a local scale has a greater chance of success when it is built within a global framework that supports it.

In addition to a change in attitude, modern peace also demands structural reforms, but such reforms are not guaranteed and can result from the erosion of the nation-state's clout within the relevant institutions. (This process has already been initiated by the onset of globalization, though less so within the framework of international institutions.) Weakened states are making important decisions and generally expressing narrow self-interests. To combat the limits of such an approach, international institutions dealing with peace and development can create a realistic peace coalition to help modernize peace and ensure its sustainability.

The United Nations—the parliament of nations—is the central body through which many reforms can begin. One potential restructuring involves the creation of an upper and lower house within the United Nations. The UN General Assembly can become the upper house, maintaining its general authorities and functions, while the lower house can comprise the mayors of the one hundred fifty most populous cities in the world. This glocalized lower house can debate global, peace-related economic, social, and cultural issues, taking on an advisory role to the assembly and bringing the decision-making process closer to the interests of citizens. The lower house can convene biannually.

A **peace and security council** can operate parallel to the UN Security Council, convening approximately four times a year on issues of peacemaking, at the discretion of the secretary general. This council represents a way to promote inclusive and participatory decision making from many spheres. It can involve the fifteen members of the UN Security Council; the heads of the fifteen largest and most active international NGOs, as selected by a committee of elder statesmen named by the secretary general; a representative of the World Bank; and representatives of peace-oriented foundations. This council, operating in an advisory capacity to the UN Security Council, can provide a balanced, multisector approach to peacemaking on a global scale.

The G-8 also can amend its agenda to include issues relating to peace and peace-related ventures. By inviting relevant institutions such as local governments, NGOs, and business leaders to participate in this agenda, the G-8 can promote values of social inclusion and can legitimize the prioritizing of peacebuilding in the international arena.

The current mandate of UN peacekeeping forces is often limited, resulting in occasionally dramatic lapses, such as the impotence of the UN Assistance Mission for Rwanda in 1994. Nonetheless, peacekeeping forces have the potential to represent a more holistic approach to peacemaking, and their mandate can be expanded to include peacebuilding activities. This reform would require the recruitment of development and peace experts to work with the post-conflict parties on joint peacebuilding projects. Such a function would parallel the peacekeeping function, contributing to cooperation between former enemies and the additional involvement of regional actors.

Separating development from peacebuilding is artificial and erroneous. If the World Bank, the biggest international development agency, works with the United Nations to operate parallel units of development and peacebuilding, lasting peace will have a greater chance of success.

A research institute linked to the United Nations, such as the International Peace Institute, can help measure and steer peace ecology by conducting ongoing research into attitudes about peace and living conditions in post-conflict zones. Such systematic research can compose the peace ecology yardstick, or peace barometer.

A formal body of youth representatives from all member states can contribute to glocalization and the evolution of an empowered international youth community. The establishment of a youth council at the United Nations—responsible for debating an agenda for the future and submitting a yearly report to the general assembly and the security council—can serve not only to train young peace diplomats but also to encourage and empower youth to influence the international agenda, both generally and on specific peace issues. The engagement of youth in the international arena has a great deal of potential as a catalyst for change.

Ultimately, it is in the international community's best interests to implement reforms toward a new peacemaking model. The international community will benefit from improved global security and stability; economies will grow and regions will be less likely to be upset by massive power imbalances.

The modern edifice of peace rests on the four pillars and reflects the principles of cooperation, vision, and peaceful values. Peace and conflict are functions not only of politics but also of human nature, of the human battle for power versus the need to connect societies for the preservation and development of life itself. Modern peace espouses life and social growth, inviting us to move past our limitations in pursuit of greater humanitarian ideals.

PART IV

On the Ground

Pax Mediterraneo

Why the Mediterranean?

BY NOW IT SHOULD BE EVIDENT THAT A MODERNIZED PEACE strategy is urgently needed to reflect today's reality and tomorrow's challenges. In the first three parts of this book I presented a concrete framework for a modern peace built on the four pillars of participatory peace and glocalization, peace ecology, peacebuilding, and creative diplomacy. We have looked at examples that demonstrate some of these ideas in action and have explored ways of integrating the four pillars into the modern peace process.

Now it's time to put these theories into practice. This final section presents an in-depth case study of modernized peacemaking in the Mediterranean Basin, a Pax Mediterraneo. After an introduction to the region, I offer a vision for peace built on the four pillars of modern peace. Particularly useful for practitioners in the field of peace and conflict studies, the Pax Mediterraneo proposes revolutionary but attainable measures for achieving lasting peace in the Mediterranean area.

Why the Mediterranean? For one, it is a highly visible region with a history of the birth of civilizations and complicated conflicts. In addition, the region continues to struggle with issues of war and peace, poverty and prosperity, immigration, and the region's relationship to the global order.

It also is the region with which I have the most direct experience, both in the peace and conflict arena and in issues of immigration and socioeconomic development. The Peres Center for Peace is currently involved in a project that aims to bring Mediterranean countries together in regional cooperation and peaceful development. The Pax Mediterraneo I offer in this book was first presented through the Peres Center in the context of the Leo Savir Foundation for a Mediterranean Vision 2020, and it has been expanded and updated here for widespread dissemination. Because the Peres Center has already begun implementing peace activities in the Mediterranean, I can speak with confidence about the immense potential for success.

Finally, I have chosen the Mediterranean as the subject of this extended case study because it is becoming the region whose destiny is most likely to influence peace on a global scale. As both a hotbed for Islamic terrorism affecting the West and a region that espouses economic progress, the Mediterranean represents a crucial intersection between the hostilities of the past and hopes for the future. Its ties with the United States, the European Union, the Middle East, and North Africa make it uniquely suited to affect peace beyond its boundaries.

My greatest hope for this Pax Mediterraneo is that it will move from the page to reality. The recommendations put forward here are not beyond the realm of possibility. Rather, they represent the steps we absolutely must take in the direction of modern peace, not only in the Mediterranean region but also in conflict regions worldwide. Although exact activities must be tailored to each region's situation, the model of the Pax Mediterraneo can and should be duplicated for peacemaking efforts across the globe.

CHAPTER 14

Peace in the Mediterranean Basin: What Will It Take?

THE MEDITERRANEAN IS A REGION OF CONTRAST: VISIONS OF blue waters and white sand set a backdrop for ethnic conflict and Maghrebian mayhem. Some of the region's richest countries lie across the water from some of the poorest. To appreciate the cultural, political, anthropological, religious, and historical diversity inherent in this area, one simply needs to look at a map: the countries that border the Mediterranean Sea range from France, Spain, and Italy to Algeria, Tunisia, and Morocco; from Israel, Greece, and Turkey to Libya, Syria, and Lebanon. There are twenty-two states along the shoreline, all of which have unique and interwoven histories and cultures.

The first step in any effort toward regional peace must be to unearth the unifying factors among these societies. The identification of common values and experiences will provide a foundation for cross-border understanding and mutual respect for human rights.

A Region of Commonalities, a Region of Conflict

The Mediterranean is rich in culture and history, relaxed in nature, full of unique flavors and cuisines, and a source of creativity. The most obvious commonality among Mediterranean societies—aside from geography—is monotheism. The Mediterranean Basin is the birthplace of Islam, Christianity, and Judaism, and the civilizations built around these religions have spread similar yet distinctive cultures throughout the region.

The Mediterranean is a source of peace and Western civilization, according to our history books. Philosophy, democracy, and humanity—as we in the West perceive them today—can be traced back to the ancient cultures of Jerusalem, Alexandria, Athens, and Rome. The modern concept of glocalization is in fact rooted in ancient Mediterranean beliefs and values: the Greek philosopher Diogenes famously claimed to be "a citizen of the world" at the time when city-states emerged.[1] Diogenes' notion of what it means to be cosmopolitan reflects the aim of modern peace to reconcile and respect local identities while also taking advantage of global opportunities.

At the core of the cosmopolitan worldview is the belief that all human beings, regardless of race, religion, gender, or political affiliation, do (or at least can) belong to a single community—a community that should be appreciated and cultivated. Just as ancient Greece saw the rise of the city-state, today's Mediterranean community can engender the rise of a decentralized peace. The Mediterranean boasts a rich history, complex philosophy, common values, and the universal desire to end war. It thus provides fertile ground on which to develop innovative ideas about peaceful coexistence beyond the narrower region of the Middle East.

But the region's commonalities often clash with the needs and desires of individual states; shared values become forgotten in the wake of conflict. Border disputes, ethno-religious violence, and civil conflicts have flared across the Mediterranean Basin despite such cooperative efforts as the Euro-Arab Dialogue, the Five + Five and Twelve + Five negotiations, and the Conference on Security and Cooperation in the Mediterranean.[2]

At the heart of Mediterranean politics lies the Israeli-Palestinian issue, the possible resolution of which will reflect on the entire region. The 2006 Hamas electoral victory in the Palestinian parliament makes the situation more difficult, but it is not an obstacle that cannot be overcome. The tools and methods of modern peace can be applied on both a country-to-country basis (for example, bilateral cooperation between Israel and Palestine) and at the regional level (the Pax Mediterraneo), thus ensuring that specific conflicts are addressed in full while also being incorporated into a larger regional framework for cooperation and peace.

The Mediterranean Proclamation: A Vision of Peace

At the outset of a Mediterranean peace process, the players can take the opportunity to outline a vision of the regional ideas about and goals for sustainable peace. The vision that the Peres Center for Peace has already proposed—to widen support among regional actors—is succinct yet powerful, balancing the ideals of modern peace with specific recommendations for practical implementation.

Glocalization: Cities and Youth

- Developing decentralized cooperation through the creation of a **network of cities** in the region that will work together on socioeconomic and cultural issues through the involvement of local governments and civil societies.

- Emphasizing **youth empowerment** and facilitating youth events and exchange.

Peace Ecology: Human Rights and Peace Education

- Developing **mutual understanding, respect, and a sense of equality** and justice, with a sensibility about disparities in size, population, and levels of development, as well as the great wealth of cultural diversity among communities. Promoting peace education, cultural exchange, and interfaith dialogue to engender an ecology of peace in the region.

- Upholding the **principles of peace**, pluralism, rule of law, human rights, equality of opportunity and development, territorial and demographic integrity, and the right to self-determination in strengthening relations among communities.

Peacebuilding: Joint Economic, Social, and Environmental Ventures

- Creating full **diplomatic, cultural, and commercial relations** among all Mediterranean countries, including exploration of federative relations between some countries.

- Creating **shared responsibility** for preserving the environment of the region, to enhance the quality of life for present and future generations and to ensure that the Mediterranean Sea, as the common natural treasure and resource, is clean of pollution.

- Taking advantage of **opportunities presented by globalization,** including rehabilitation after conflict; strengthening regional cooperation and integration; creation of a regional financial mechanism and establishment of free trade zones, both independently and with the European Union and the United States; and bridging economic divides within and beyond national borders by facilitating free movement of people and goods and by developing joint infrastructures for water (including canals), communication, energy, transportation, tourism, high technology, integrated crop management, and desert habitation.

Creative Diplomacy: Borders, Security, and the International Community

- **Resolving conflicts and rejecting violence** in an effort to move toward a just peace that will inspire cooperation and foster a common identity and future throughout the region. Conflicts will end through creative diplomacy, based on equality, and border disputes can be handled according to international resolutions, security arrangements, and the principle of territory for peace.

- Promoting nonviolent resolution of all issues of contention by employing creative diplomacy according to **shared current and future interests.**

- Creating a pact against all forms of violence, and cooperating in the struggle against terrorism and for the **enhancement of security arrangements.**

- Creating a comprehensive Mediterranean peacebuilding framework, such as a **Mediterranean Partnership for Peace** with NATO (patterned on the Eastern European model), that is based on cooperation and dialogue about political, socioeconomic, and cultural issues at all levels.

- Cooperating with the **international community,** including the United States, the European Union, Russia, Japan, the United Nations, and the World Bank, to strengthen the Pax Mediterraneo in all aspects of cooperation, including peacebuilding, decentralized peace, the promotion of a peace ecology, peacekeeping, and security arrangements.

This Mediterranean Proclamation can be the starting point for a more detailed discussion of Mediterranean peace. After all parties have committed to its principles, the proclamation represents a skeletal structure for the Pax Mediterraneo, which can be initiated by regional actors and orchestrated with the help of the United States and of the European Union, the southern states of which are part of the Mediterranean region. The proclamation can be thought of as the mission statement, whereas the Pax Mediterraneo is the business plan.

The primary aims of the Pax Mediterraneo are to develop a joint Mediterranean identity, to endow each state with a sense of belonging to the greater region, and to serve as the basis for modern peacemaking. The Pax Mediterraneo can be the focus of a Mediterranean peace summit at which national and regional players agree on roles and responsibilities in the implementation of the outlined activities.

Implementation, however, comes later. My goal here is to offer a structure for creating a Pax Mediterraneo that covers all elements of the Mediterranean Proclamation and that is built on the four pillars of modern peace, which are represented in the remaining four chapters of this book. Each chapter offers specific, practical guidance for implementing that pillar's concepts in the Mediterranean. These tools and methods also can be shaped to suit the needs of other areas and conflicts worldwide.

The proclamation and the Pax Mediterraneo that I present here are not, of course, set in stone. However, these recommendations have been shaped by years of experience and successful implementation, and I present them as a foundation on which Mediterranean peace can be built. The successful implementation of a Pax Mediterraneo can guide regional cooperation and relationships during the peacemaking process and well into the future.

CHAPTER 15

Cities and Youth

THIS SECTION OF THE PAX MEDITERRANEO EXPLAINS HOW TO take advantage of a city's unique position among Mediterranean nations and within the region as a whole. I also offer concrete mechanisms through which the region's youth can become active participants in the peacemaking process. Ultimately, the goal of glocalization is to invite the participation of people from all sectors of Mediterranean society and from conflict, post-conflict, and peaceful countries.

City-to-City Networking

Participatory peace in the Mediterranean can start with the establishment of a network of coastal cities—particularly in conflict and post-conflict zones—that would work together toward interdependence. A decentralized peace will enable a more equitable distribution of peace dividends across the social strata. The international community, possibly through a Madrid II or Annapolis II conference, could declare its support for decentralization based on expanding urbanization and the growing importance of the city in international affairs.

In a May 2005 Memorandum of Understanding between the World Bank and the Glocal Forum, the World Bank reaffirmed its commitment to "continue to provide support" for the Forum's activities. That commitment represents financial, logistical, and training support as well as support for the Glocal Youth Parliament, which "facilitates the involvement of GYP parliamentarians in World Bank youth meetings and programs"; the City Diplomacy program, which "develops and implements decentralized initiatives between cities to promote cooperative relations toward development and peacebuilding"; and the We Are the Future children's centers that have been established in Africa and the Middle East.[1]

With the continued support of the World Bank and other international actors, the Glocal Forum and other like-minded organizations can explore glocalization activities in the broader Mediterranean region, the core Middle East area, and the Israeli-Palestinian context. Decentralized peace within the broader Mediterranean region can be based on a Euro-Mediterranean model supported by the European Union. Through this model, cities can work together on building the capacity to address growing urbanization. A Mediterranean city gateway portal—an online database and forum—can offer mayors and municipalities a channel for exchanging best practices and facilitating economic cooperation, including joint procurement, which can potentially enhance a city's buying power.

In the Middle East core region, intercity relations can be shaped by cultural and heritage tourism. There presently are twenty-five UNESCO-listed heritage sites in Egypt, Israel, Jordan, Lebanon, the Palestinian Authority, and Syria.[2] These countries and sites share a Middle Eastern Mediterranean culture, but they also vary greatly. Through city-to-city cooperation, their geographical, political, and cultural peculiarities can transcend state borders. Cooperation will require local tourism agencies (as well as accommodation and transportation infrastructures) to work together and coordinate an archeological tour, providing knowledge and understanding of the differing cultures and histories of the participating nations. The tour could be marketed toward American, European, and Asian travelers.

Cooperation among countries and cities on behalf of our common natural treasures can inspire both a sense of identification and a sense of shared destiny. Such cooperation not only will enhance regional environmental resources and advance tourism but also will serve as an impetus for peaceful coexistence. To achieve these aims, projects can be created and implemented that involve the following port cities:

- **Middle East:** Al'Aqabah, Jordan; Alexandria, Egypt; Ashdod, Israel; Beirut, Lebanon; Gaza City, Palestinian Authority; and Latakia, Syria

- **Maghreb:** Algiers, Algeria; Casablanca, Morocco; Tripoli, Libya; and Tunis, Tunisia

- **Southern Europe:** Barcelona, Spain; Istanbul, Turkey; Limassol, Cyprus; Marseille, France; Naples, Italy; Thessaloníki, Greece; and Valletta, Malta

- **Balkans:** Bar, Montenegro; Durrës, Albania; Izola, Slovenia; Mostar, Bosnia and Herzegovina (not a seaside city, but the closest big city to the shore); and Split, Croatia

The creation of cross-border tours based on city-to-city interaction could enhance cooperation among cultural policy makers, local authorities, heritage circles, and tourism professionals, with a focus on translating concepts into concrete policy and activity. In this way, people from many walks of life would be able to participate in the peace process. Coordination with regional institutions, particularly with the ministries of tourism of the Middle Eastern countries, will extend the cooperation to other areas. More cooperative environmental and tourism ventures are discussed in chapter 17.

Decentralized peacemaking should be most intense in the Israeli-Palestinian context. City networks can be chosen according to their proximity, nature, and potential contribution to the participatory peace process. Cities outside the Middle East can complete the peace triangles and facilitate cooperation. For example, these city triangles can include Nablus–Rishon Le-Zion–Barcelona; Jericho-Caesarea-Athens; Ramallah–Tel Aviv–Lyon; Tulkarm-Netanya-Istanbul; Qalqilya–Kfar Saba–Naples; Jenin-Afula-Marseille; and Bethlehem-Beersheba-Rome.

Cooperation can begin with cultural exchange and capacity building for urban governance. Mayors can interact directly with their cross-border counterparts on issues of trade, tourism, culture, sports, youth projects, urban planning, the environment, and rural-urban integration. The third, international cities can host representatives from the two post-conflict cities for training sessions within these domains.

Youth Empowerment

Today's youth—tomorrow's adults—must embrace peace as a central objective and acknowledge that peace offers everyone the best and only option for a brighter future. The imaginative and educational approach to youth empowerment taken by the Peres Center for Peace and the Glocal Forum has been designed to alter negative stereotypes and instill positive perceptions, thereby encouraging communication between former enemies and ultimately establishing peaceful coexistence.

As agents of change, young people transcend all elements of peacemaking and can penetrate psychological boundaries adults cannot. The older generation of politicians is often too set in its ways and frozen in its hostilities to engender necessary change. With their idealism and open-minded approaches, young people can contribute enormously to projects in glocalization, peace ecology, and peacebuilding. Governments can invite youth to be active members of the peacemaking process by creating a Mediterranean Youth Forum aimed at bringing together youth from conflict, post-conflict, and other areas in pursuit of peace.

The Mediterranean Youth Forum can target high school–age youth from seashore cities in the Mediterranean region. Youth can be recruited for the forum through a competition implemented by local municipalities—for example, a competition to express a vision of peace in the Mediterranean for the year 2020. The winning candidates from each city will participate in the Mediterranean Youth

Forum, which can set a framework for a Mediterranean youth parliament and draft a regional youth agenda for 2020.

The forum will facilitate intercultural exchange and will enhance mutual understanding, tolerance, and the breaking down of stereotypes in Mediterranean conflict regions. The participatory nature of the forum also will serve to overcome distorted and even racist stereotypes that have recently surfaced as a result of globalization and the immigration of citizens from southern Mediterranean to northern Mediterranean countries. The youth parliament will evolve into a steering committee to be consulted on youth projects throughout the peace process and thereafter.

Facilitation of the Mediterranean Youth Forum and Youth Agenda 2020 will require the full involvement of municipalities. To bring the youth agenda to a local level, the winning competitors from each municipality can establish local youth councils, which would interact frequently with mayors and bureaucracies and, more importantly, with the other Mediterranean youth councils established by the Glocal Forum. This comprehensive project—entailing creative expression, dialogue, and cultural exchange as well as the creation of a youth agenda, a youth parliament, and local youth councils—integrates the notions of glocalization, peace ecology, and peacebuilding. In this vein, youth from the United States can play an important role in encouraging Mediterranean interaction within the region and in the larger international community. At last, youth can be put on the front lines of peace rather than the front lines of war.

CHAPTER 16

Human Rights and Peace Education

AS WE HAVE LEARNED, CONFLICT AND POST-CONFLICT SOCIETIES are often trapped in a culture of war in which anger, suspicion, and blame fuel a mind-set of hostility toward the Other. Even peaceful societies can experience this attitude toward neighboring countries, regardless of whether there is violence between them. In the Mediterranean Basin, tensions are common between countries in the Middle East, North Africa, and southern Europe, and even among peaceful European countries. It is therefore crucial to address comprehensive peacemaking in the Mediterranean on a psychological level—to change the ecology of peace.

The Pax Mediterraneo can first approach peace ecology by using a peace barometer to study current attitudes toward peacemaking. Thereafter, the Pax Mediterraneo can integrate human rights, media campaigns, and intercultural exchange into an overall agenda that heightens the level of peace education in the Mediterranean region.

Peace Barometer

An independent group can be recruited to conduct a survey of attitudes toward peace in the Mediterranean region. As an example, I've included an excerpt from an actual peace barometer for Israel and Palestine, based on Gallup International surveys dated December 2005 to January 2006. The questions posed in this Israeli-Palestinian peace barometer provide a solid foundation for questions and issues that can be addressed in a regional peace barometer.

Peace Barometer: Israel and Palestine

1. War and Peace

How would you rate the quality of relationship between Israelis and Palestinians?

	POSITIVE	NEUTRAL	NEGATIVE
Palestinians	12%	22%	61%
Israelis	9%	24%	65%

In essence, do you support the peace process?

	YES	NO
Palestinians	64%	31%
Israelis	81%	17%

In your opinion, how can self-determination be achieved for your people? Do you believe in a nonviolent process or in violent struggle?

	NONVIOLENT	VIOLENT
Palestinians	53%	27%
Israelis	69%	16%

Do you prefer peaceful coexistence, despite disagreements with the other side, or suffering and looking to the future?

	COEXISTENCE	SUFFERING
Palestinians	41%	32%
Israelis	51%	26%

2. Vision and Identity

In your opinion, will peace ever exist between Israelis and Palestinians?

	YES	NO
Palestinians	22%	60%
Israelis	26%	60%

In your opinion, are the chances high or low for achieving permanent peace arrangements?

	HIGH	LOW
Palestinians	21%	72%
Israelis	24%	71%

Do you believe that the world is advancing toward peace or conflict?

	PEACE	CONFLICT
Palestinians	20%	65%
Israelis	46%	34%

3. Creative Diplomacy (for Arab/Israeli–bordering countries only)

Do you support the notion of dividing Jerusalem by applying joint sovereignty to holy sites?

	YES	NO
Palestinians	23%	58%
Israelis	25%	61%

4. Economic Cooperation

Do you believe in a Mediterranean Union that would unify the countries surrounding the Mediterranean Sea, similar to the European Union?

	YES	NO
Palestinians	25%	49%
Israelis	36%	48%

5. Peace Ecology

Are you for or against peace education curriculum at school?

	FOR	AGAINST
Palestinians	47%	42%
Israelis	73%	19%

Clearly, according to this data, Israeli and Palestinian public opinions about peace process–related issues are similar. Both societies prefer a nonviolent peace process to a violent struggle, and both believe in the need for peaceful coexistence rather than in the continuation of suffering (even if the latter will produce more desirable results in the long run). However, neither of the parties believes in the possibility of peaceful coexistence or the chance for an arrangement. Both sides refer negatively to the other, and they do not recognize the value of economic interrelationship—yet both societies believe in the need for a peace education curriculum, which makes our case for the necessity of peace ecology.

I believe these attitudes are mirrored in the Mediterranean region at large, which is why a comprehensive approach to peace ecology is essential. Making the transition from a culture of war to a culture of peace requires a holistic view of peacemaking, including peace education, from the treatment of identity on a national level to personal exchanges between citizens of conflict states.

Human Rights

Peace ecology is not about forcing homogeneity where none exists; it is about celebrating common values and beliefs while recognizing and respecting the differences between societies. Peace ecology must be based on a fundamental respect for human rights and a belief in the equality of people, regardless of nationality or religion. To appreciate the commonalities between people, we must first accept that we are all of equal worth and that our basic human rights are sacred.

The concept of human rights has been addressed in the highest echelons of the international community, most concretely in the UN's Universal Declaration of Human Rights (1948),[1] the Office of the High Commissioner for Human Rights, and the Human Rights Council. With the guidance of the Universal Declaration and the two UN groups, a Mediterranean human rights association can be established to further civil and political rights in the region and to work with local NGOs to preserve the human rights of local citizens.

If Mediterranean countries commit to principles of peace, pluralism, human rights, territorial and demographic integrity, and the right to self-determination in strengthening relationships among communities, the region will make great strides toward decentralizing peace. Clear links exist between democratization and peace, but they cannot be imposed upon regimes and should evolve out of grassroots processes.

In other words, human rights cannot simply be a set of rules imposed from above—it must also be an organic concept that is nurtured within each citizen in the region. The Pax Mediterraneo offers methods of recruiting the media as well as local and regional leaders into the campaign for peace based on equality.

Media Campaigns

First and foremost, the rhetoric of leaders must reflect the basic values of peace—mutual respect, justice, and above all, equality. Only a peace informed by these values can lead to genuine reconciliation. Regional and international players can assist in creating this environment through the press and other media.

One example of a media campaign for peace could be a series of programs called Children of Abraham. The campaign could be guided by the joint public relations committee (as described in chapter 12) together with governmental groups and private institutions from both the core conflict area and the broader Mediterranean region. The campaign could address the value of peace, emphasizing the younger generation. By highlighting the proximities of Jewish and Arab religions, histories, and cultures, the campaign can bring today's children of Abraham together within the common framework of their roots and their connection to the land. With an aggressive and emotional campaign, stressing the importance of childhood development against a background of the trauma and horrors facing children in conflict societies, people on both sides of the Israeli-Palestinian border and in neighboring countries can recognize that children's lives can only be improved through peace.

The media can also be recruited to illustrate cross-border encounters between young people, reflecting the optimism of the younger generation. Such shows can be formatted within existing structures, such as MTV, and produced by a Mediterranean station (RAI, TVE, or TF1) with the participation of local media avenues. The contents of these and other public relations campaigns must condemn the forces that pursue conflict in the name of nationalism.

Media to Media

The media's depiction of the peace process is pivotal to the cultivation of a peace ecology. All too often, the media assumes that conflict sells and that consumers are accustomed to the vilification of the former enemy. The ignorance of journalists and their desire to sell news often result in aggressive, negative media coverage of the peace process and of relations between the parties. To overcome these obstacles, credible and influential Mediterranean media outlets—such as Spain's *El Pais,* France's *Le Monde,* and Italy's RAI—can host forums for journalists from the Mediterranean region, specifically from core conflict or post-conflict areas such as the Middle East and the Balkans. These forums can facilitate the exchange of methodologies and enhance understanding of the other side.

The forums also can provide the basis for joint syndication of the print media and joint production of their electronic counterparts. For example, exchange of technology and journalists between Middle Eastern newspapers—including *Yedioth Ahronoth* from Tel Aviv, *Al-Quds* from the Palestinian Authority, *Al-Ra'i* from Amman, *Dar Al-Hayat* (the most widely read Arabic newspaper in the world), and *Al-Baath* and *Tishreen* from Damascus—can promote cross-border cooperation and a deeper understanding of former enemies. TV channels also can be recruited for such a mission, including LBC from Lebanon, Al-Jazeera from Saudi Arabia, Channel 2 from Israel, and Persian Gulf television.

The media should not merely show the peace process through rose-colored glasses; it should strive to paint a realistic picture of the process, the former enemy, the struggle to coexist, and the real issues that pervade the atmosphere. Nationalist media coverage can become a phenomenon of the past.

Intercultural Exchanges

In addition to public campaigning, direct interaction between former enemies is an important part of nurturing mutual understanding and creating a common language. Cross-border cultural exchanges—in theater, film, painting, literature, and dance—and exposure to a neighbor's creative identity can help engender understanding and respect. These exchanges might include joint theater groups with writers from both sides of the border; joint exhibitions of photography or art, potentially relating to perceptions of war and peace; and joint film productions—perhaps the most crucial media, because movies reach the broadest audience. A Mediterranean film fund could support joint movie productions, with assistance from Hollywood, if possible. Such an effort is currently under way with the involvement of major players from Hollywood, Europe, Israel, and the Palestinian Authority, under the name of Zoora Media.

Interfaith dialogue is another integral element of cultural exchange and the broader peace concept. The Mediterranean is the birthplace of the three monotheistic religions—Christianity, Judaism, and Islam. Islamic religious leaders are often conservative, fearing that peace will lead to "dangerous" openness and westernization, whereas Western religious leaders perceive Islam as violent and oppressive. Each side is ignorant of and lacks respect for the other's culture. Intercultural and interfaith dialogues are therefore crucial to heightening tolerance and promoting mutual understanding among Mediterranean cultures.

Rome, the home of the Vatican, could host a forum of Mediterranean religious representatives to promote tolerance, cultural exchange, interfaith dialogue, and peaceful coexistence in the name of religion. As of this writing, the Peres Center for Peace and the Glocal Forum are planning one such interfaith program, scheduled for May 2008 in Rome, which will bring together leaders from the three monotheistic religions and political leaders such as the king of Morocco, the president of Israel, and the president of the Palestinian Authority. The meeting will take place in the Ara Pacis, the ancient temple of the emperor of peace, Augustus, and will be followed up by interfaith and intercultural dialogue.

War in the name of religion has been launched too many times, and many of the terrorist activities in the region are still fueled by religious extremism. It is time that organized religion and the Biblical scriptures were used to promote peace instead of war.

Cultivating a peace ecology in the Mediterranean will demand a push on many fronts—media campaigns, cultural exchanges, and interfaith dialogues—to effect the necessary change in public opinion. That change will not be easy, but when these and other projects gain traction, the momentum will spread to other areas of peacemaking as well. It is important to tackle peacemaking from many angles, on many levels, and with the participation of as many players as possible if we want to support real, lasting peace.

CHAPTER SEVENTEEN

Joint Economic, Social, Environmental, and Tourism Ventures

THIS SECTION OF THE PAX MEDITERRANEO OUTLINES SPE-cific projects that can help develop national and regional economies, build infrastructure, and protect the environment of the Mediterranean region. The purpose of these projects is to connect Mediterranean countries with one another physically, financially, and socially, thus providing the literal and metaphoric framework in which peace can develop. The projects I present here are but a few examples of the ventures that can be included in a Mediterranean peace agreement.

Before peacebuilding ventures can begin, formal relations between all parties must be established to open up channels of communication that were previously silent. Egypt is the only Arab country along the Mediterranean coastline that has formal diplomatic relations with Israel. With the advancement of a formal peace process, Israel should be able to establish formal diplomatic relations with Algeria, Lebanon, Libya, Morocco, Syria, Tunisia, and eventually, with the future Palestine. Initially, diplomatic relationships can involve exchanges of envoys, to be eventually upgraded to exchanges of ambassadors upon final negotiations of border disputes. Israeli commercial and cultural institutions can be represented in Algiers, Beirut, Damascus, Ramallah, and Tripoli. Corresponding Arab representation can be stationed in Tel Aviv until the question of Jerusalem is resolved.

With formal relations in place, Mediterranean countries can come together to establish an overall development framework for peacebuilding projects within conflict and post-conflict societies. The focus of peacebuilding should be the equitable distribution of peace dividends—that is, the economic growth and increased standard of living for all segments of society that should come with peace.

Peacebuilding projects in the Pax Mediterraneo fall broadly into four categories: economic, social, environmental, and tourism ventures. To best support cooperation, all projects can incorporate joint activity on the part of at least two societies—forging connections that may previously have been tenuous or nonexistent.

Economic Ventures

The economic element of the Pax Mediterraneo can outline joint peacebuilding projects that aim to develop cross-border infrastructure and to narrow the socioeconomic gaps between poor and rich nations. The Mediterranean Basin is a typically heterogeneous neighborhood, comprising a prosperous north, a developing south, and struggling economies in between, as evidenced in Figure 1.

To help balance these figures, a regional economy can be developed that emphasizes the involvement of post-conflict economies and the Middle East. A group of donors led by the United States, the European Union, Japan, Canada, the World Bank, the IMF, the United Nations, and other regional actors can outline the goals and methodologies of the regional economy, as well as the rehabilitation of post-conflict economies—a sort of Marshall Plan for the Mediterranean. Rehabilitation can deal with the refurbishment of infrastructures destroyed during war, the planning of a socially inclusive peace economy that highlights unemployment and narrows the socioeconomic gap, and the free movement of goods and people. Seven of the twenty-two Mediterranean nations are members of the European Union; these seven countries can provide expert economic guidance, regional funding mechanisms, and other support for the development of the regional economy.

In addition to the international donor group, a committee of Israeli, Palestinian, and Jordanian representatives could be established to explore a federative economic arrangement, outlining a

Figure 1: GDP per capita in US dollars[1]

COUNTRY	GDP PER CAPITA
France	$33,800
Spain	$33,700
Italy	$31,000
Israel	$28,800
Lebanon	$10,400
Turkey	$9,400
Tunisia	$7,500
Bosnia and Herzegovina	$6,600
Egypt	$5,400
Syria	$4,500
Morocco	$3,800
Gaza Strip and West Bank	$1,100

free trade area among them that eventually would be extended to the European Union and the United States. The committee would work with local finance ministries to monitor the gradual implementation of this arrangement.

One of the major focuses of peacebuilding projects should be the equitable distribution of resources. The Mediterranean region is rich in resources, but distribution remains uneven. Water has been a cause of worldwide political conflict for decades, particularly in regions that face water shortages, and the Middle East is no exception. However, water also can serve to enhance relationships instead of straining them; water sharing can be a foundation for political, economic, strategic, and geopolitical arrangements between states. Each diplomatic agreement between Mediterranean states should be accompanied by a water-sharing clause.

Water as a natural resource is integral to many elements of life—health, agriculture, economy, electricity, sanitation, cooling systems, recreation, tourism, fishing, and sewage all depend on water to some degree. However, water is finite and must therefore be managed for sustainable, equitable use. The Mediterranean encompasses regions that are rich in water and forests and those that are thirsty, desert areas. Accordingly, water activity in the Mediterranean Basin can be administered in different ways, depending on the circumstances of the area.

Initially, the establishment of a water database can enhance water cooperation among all Mediterranean countries. Such a database can help manage the implementation of water-related clauses in the Convention for the Protection of the Mediterranean Sea against Pollution (1976), also known as the Barcelona Convention.[2] In addition, seashore cities can exchange information and cooperate on activities regarding water supply, desalination, sanitation, and sewage-purification systems (including their future agricultural usefulness in solving water shortages).

On a regional level, water activity can be both strategic and economic. Activities can include management of joint water resources (rivers, groundwater, drainage basins, etc.), conditional on the interests and circumstances of each country; the establishment of a decision-making system for water resources, similarly based on strategic and economic considerations; and analysis of common projects.

On a national level, water activities can be based on neighborly relations and common borders. Projects will be more concrete because of proximity and because of the parties' mutual geographical and economic dependence on the available resource. One example is the potential cooperation between Israel and its neighbors: use of the northern Dead Sea springs, removal and utilization of sewage in the western zones of the West Bank, utilization of sewage in East Jerusalem, and connection of Gaza to desalination operations in Ashkelon. One water-sharing project currently on the table is the digging of a Red Sea/Dead Sea canal, which is being spearheaded by King Abdullah II of Jordan, President Peres of Israel, and President Abu Mazen of the Palestinian Authority. The success of this peacebuilding project will surely pave the way for similar resource-sharing projects in the future.

Related to water sharing, agricultural ventures—including integrated crop management, modern irrigation system management, and peri-urban agricultural development—can greatly enhance economies and cooperation between Mediterranean states. For example, Israel and Palestine can share technology and agricultural knowledge through joint farms and production facilities. Agricultural trade opportunities with Europe, Asia, North America, and the Persian Gulf states can be maximized through joint marketing. A similar but more limited cooperation can take place among Israel, Jordan, Lebanon, and Syria, particularly in the border regions. For example, hothouses may be developed in the Jordan Valley and in southern Lebanon and innovative crops may be grown on the Golan Heights and in northern Galilee.

Another opportunity for economic and industrial cooperation is the regional use of solar energy. The world is quickly running out of conventional fuel, and alternative energy sources have become a critical field. Recent years have seen a technological breakthrough in the field of solar research known as concentrator photovoltaics.[3] The idea is to take small, highly efficient solar cells and then concentrate sunlight onto them using large mirrors or lenses. This produces a great deal more electricity from each solar cell than would be possible if the cell were simply exposed to direct sunlight, and thus reduces their effective cost per watt. Solar technology has reached a stage where large solar power plants could be constructed as cost-effectively as conventional fossil-fueled plants.

Radiation from the sun could be converted to low-cost electricity to power electrolysis units. It also could be used to extract hydrogen from seawater, with oxygen as a waste product. That hydrogen could then be used to fuel trucks, cars, and even planes, producing pure water vapor as waste.[4] If countries could generate their own pollution-free (hydrogen) fuel from low-grade water, and in the process of burning that fuel create pure water as a byproduct, the benefits would be not only environmental but also political. The use of independent sources of fuel rather than imported fuel could lead to an entirely new and healthier order of national priorities for all the countries concerned.

The total estimated population for all countries around the Mediterranean Basin was 462 million people in 2005. A 150 kilometer by 150 kilometer solar megaplant located in the Sahara could provide electricity for the entire population of the Mediterranean Basin, at a per capita level in excess of 8,000 kilowatt-hours per year.[5] This figure almost equals the per capita output requirement in France. Initiating such a program, however, requires decisions regarding cooperation and investment—hence the need to address these issues within the framework of the Pax Mediterraneo.

Information technology can enhance the effectiveness, transparency, and accessibility of peacebuilding activities. For example, an online Mediterranean city gateway portal can be established, in conjunction with the Euro-Mediterranean Partnership, to provide an interactive forum for professional groups and peacebuilding initiatives in the region. Information technology could also facilitate a forum to initiate e-commerce projects between post-conflict countries, which would take advantage of the knowledge and language skills each side has to offer. Technological capabilities represent one of the most important resources a country can possess in today's globalized world; the exchange of knowledge in this field is therefore a crucial part of bringing lesser developed countries on par with richer countries in the region.

Social Ventures

Joint social programs are an integral part of peacebuilding activities, particularly in the realms of health and sports. These activities can be guided by the joint committee for peacebuilding.

The nourishment of children is an important element of peacemaking in post-conflict environments, where many children under the age of six suffer malnutrition. Coordination of the international community with local peacebuilding activities can provide these children with much-needed vitamins. Peace is about living and enhancing quality of life, and food security for children—the future leaders of society—is the essence of peace.

One example of a joint health program in the Israeli-Palestinian region could be an agreement allowing Palestinian children access to Israeli health services, financed by the international community. The program could include the opportunity for Palestinian physicians to be trained alongside their Israeli counterparts, and for Israeli and Palestinian hospitals to be linked through a telemedicine apparatus that facilitates cross-border access to information on diagnoses, treatment methods, and surgical remedies. This interactive health forum also can be extended to research and development institutions, such as medical faculties in universities. The Peres Center for Peace is currently running a Saving Children program, financed by Italy, which allows sick Palestinian children to access in Israel the medical treatment they can't get in Palestine. Other NGOs can develop similar programs in other parts of the region.

Peacebuilding projects in the arts can provide infrastructure such as music and film studios and art schools. As I discussed in chapter 16 in relation to peace ecology, joint projects in this field can create a common language between former enemies. In the area of sports, soccer stadiums and basketball courts can be built or rehabilitated and used for joint training sessions. The Mediterranean Basin can be a useful platform for such activity, allowing subregional competitions and year-round training. With time, these peace-sports activities can be institutionalized by the International Olympic Committee. A Tel Aviv–Ramallah bid for the 2020 Olympic Games may seem far-fetched, but it would demonstrate a commitment to cultivating a peaceful environment in the long term.

Another area of Mediterranean cooperation can involve strengthening cultural ties, which would emphasize cultural affinity among Mediterranean inhabitants. For example, youth from ten Mediterranean countries already have engaged in a project dedicated to drawing and writing about peace, inspired by Picasso, in cooperation with the Picasso Foundation and the Leo Savir Foundation for a Mediterranean Vision 2020 within the Peres Center for Peace. Art can be educational, stimulating, and fun, which makes it an excellent opportunity to invite youth into the peacemaking process.

Environment

The Mediterranean Sea is the heart of the countries that surround it. A shared responsibility for the environment will enhance a common Mediterranean identity at the most basic level. The preservation of the sea's coastline is a common interest of all the countries on its shores, and the vast threats to its environment should be jointly overcome by the surrounding nations.

The Mediterranean Sea forms a bridge between three major continents—Africa, Asia, and Europe—all of which contribute to and suffer from water pollution and degeneration in the sea. Beaches are overbuilt and pollutants from both land-based sources and heavy maritime traffic are contaminating the waters of the basin, much to the detriment of marine animals and shore life.

The Mediterranean also suffers from irregular rainfall, water shortages, lack of extensive fertile plains, desert areas, and natural floods. Its natural resources are not equally divided throughout the region; the southern and eastern shores, those most in need of water, suffer from frequent shortages. Approximately 80 percent of the arid areas are suffering from desertification, and increasing urban sprawl is leading to the loss of high-quality soil. More than half the Mediterranean coastline is urbanized, which has resulted in increased pollution and waste and the loss of natural habitats and forests—which in turn lead to the destruction of species and increased pressure on the water supply.[6]

All of these problems—pollution, water scarcity, desertification, and soil degradation—can be direct or indirect causes of social, political, and economic instability. In other words, the longer these problems fester, the less likely it is that a stable and comprehensive peace can be achieved.

From 1971 to 1975, increasing concerns about the declining condition of the Mediterranean led to international calls for cooperation and action. The culmination of these demands was an array of treaties and conventions signed by the rim countries in cooperative attempts to control the problems outlined above. The first of these agreements was the Barcelona Convention, which aimed to coordinate international efforts to protect the marine environment and seacoasts. The convention dealt with four main types of pollution: dumping from ships and aircraft; pollution from ships; pollution from exploration of the continental shelf, seabed, and subsoil; and pollution from land-based sources.

At that time, the Mediterranean Action Plan and its coordinating unit were established. The action plan comprises four major components: a coordinated program for research, monitoring and exchange of information and assessment of the state of pollution; development and management of the basin's resources; a framework convention and technical annexes for protection of the environment; and institutional and financial arrangements for carrying out the plan.[7]

In 1996, the Barcelona Convention was revised and again ratified by all signatories. As a result, the Mediterranean Commission on Sustainable Development was set up as an advisory body on the Mediterranean Action Plan. In addition, the Euro-Mediterranean Ministerial Conference on the Environment unanimously adopted the Short- and Medium-Term Priority Environmental Action Programme (1997), a framework of action for the protection of the Mediterranean environment within the context of the Euro-Mediterranean Partnership.[8] Priorities include integrated water, waste, and coastal zone management.

In addition to these conservation efforts, other solutions are necessary and can involve regional cooperation in all environmental arenas. The collection, dissemination, and exchange of data and information are vital to economic sustainability, regional cooperation, and ultimately, lasting peace.

Tourism

Environmental preservation not only improves the potential for economic growth in the Mediterranean but also provides a fertile foundation for increased tourism in the region. Ecotourism is one of the fastest growing segments of the tourism industry. The Holy Land also has tremendous potential for pilgrimages and other tourism to religious attractions.

Tourism in the Mediterranean is generally concentrated in the richest and most developed countries; if we direct our marketing efforts toward promotion of cross-border tourism in areas recovering from conflict, we can bring greater numbers of tourists (and more tourist dollars) to those regions desperately in need of financial support.

Tourism in post-conflict environments can create cross-border infrastructure, including roads and railways, and can open up airspace and waters. Through cooperative tourism, former enemies have the opportunity to acquire a deeper knowledge of one another, to foster understanding between their peoples, and to engage in cultural exchange that helps reduce prejudices. In the end, sympathy and understanding can lead to a diminishment of tension in the region, contribute to peace, and enhance post-conflict economies by potentially bringing millions of tourists to regions that once were too risky to visit. Ultimately, cross-border tourism can help the Mediterranean become a united and more harmonious regional community.

Joint economic, social, environmental, and tourism ventures in the Mediterranean area can bring the region's countries together in a way never seen before. Peacebuilding does not simply represent a one-way channel from rich countries to poor countries; these cooperative activities can enrich all sides through the exchange of knowledge and culture, and can present opportunities for economic and social growth that benefits developing and developed countries alike.

CHAPTER EIGHTEEN

Borders, Security, and the International Community

A DISCUSSION OF THE PAX MEDITERRANEO WOULD NOT BE complete without acknowledging the many complex and some-times seemingly insoluble conflicts in the Mediterranean region. Even the best peacebuilding plans and media campaigns will come to nothing if past tensions and conflicts continue to be exploited in negotiations and other diplomatic interactions.

Creative diplomacy invites us to step back from the narrow view of unresolved issues as potentially painful "concessions" and to view them instead as opportunities to take an innovative approach to solving problems. Creative diplomacy avoids the use of surgical tools to split assets, territories, and issues. Instead, it employs measures that espouse compromise and entrench a feeling of gain, even pride, within both communities. *Compromise* is not a dirty word, and it shouldn't be treated as such. The Pax Medi-terraneo must set the standard for thinking outside the box in an effort to satisfy the interests of both sides. In creative diplomacy, everybody wins.

In the Mediterranean—particularly in the context of the Israeli-Palestinian conflict—the areas of negotiation that need the highest level of creative diplomacy are border resolutions and comprehen-sive security arrangements. This section of the Pax Mediterraneo will be dedicated to offering innovative solutions to these seeming-ly intractable obstacles to the peace process. In the Middle East, bilateral negotiation teams can be established between Israel and Palestine, Israel and Syria, and Israel and Lebanon. The spirit of these negotiations can focus on strategizing a modern peace based on equality and respect for cultural identities, including the recognition of the Palestinian right to an independent state.

Borders

If a modern peace for the Middle East within the Mediterranean context is to be achieved, creative diplomacy will have to be applied to the hotly disputed issue of permanent borders. Here, I will focus on the Israeli-Palestinian border, including the emotionally loaded question of Jerusalem, and the Israeli-Syrian border, which contains the strategically important Golan Heights. Past negotiations regarding these borders have been rife with disagreements and "unacceptable" concessions, which is why the revolutionary approach of creative diplomacy is required, to shed new light on old problems. Instead of focusing on what each side is "losing," we must emphasize the potential gains of permanent border resolutions, including economic growth and cooperative ventures that can generate peace dividends on both sides.

Border issues can generally be resolved based on UN Security Council Resolutions 242 (1967) and 338 (1973)[1]—Israeli withdrawals from territories occupied in 1967 (the West Bank and the Golan Heights) and territory exchange for designing the blocs of settlements. Security arrangements most likely to affect issues of jurisdiction for territories adjacent to the 1967 borders can remain open to negotiation. Israel's recognition of such issues paves the way for Arab progress on issues of peace relations and security.

Rather than being demarcated by concrete blocks, deployed forces, and land mines, Israel's border with the West Bank and Gaza can comprise ten industrialized trade zones that will develop high-tech and mid-tech industries with investment from wealthier Mediterranean countries, the European Union, and the United States. The ten zones can be strategically placed adjacent to the main cities of the West Bank—Bethlehem, Jenin, Qalqilya, Ramallah, Tulkarm, and two southeast of Hebron—and in Gaza, at the Erez, Kissufim, and Rafah crossings.

The borders can more or less reflect the 1967 cease-fire lines, with the exception of four Israeli settlement blocs—Gush Etzion, Ma'ale Adumim, the Latrun region, and the Alfe Menashe region, which together make up about 3 percent of the West Bank. These four blocs can be swapped on a one-to-one ratio with territory that expands Gaza into the Negev by 169.2 square kilometers. This area can be used to house Palestinian refugees whose right to return to their new homeland—the future Palestine—will be enshrined.

There is probably no more emotionally laden issue than the political fate of Jerusalem, a city that has been conquered by civilizations and empires but has not yet seen a peaceful resolution between two nations or religions. More symbols and passions exist in Jerusalem than anywhere in the world. Since 1967, Jerusalem has been a united city under Israeli jurisdiction, but the city is split in terms of population and emotional perspective among approximately 465,000 Israeli Jews and 230,000 Arabs.[2] For Jews, Jerusalem is the heart and the magnet of the Jewish state, religion, culture, and history. For Muslims, Jerusalem is holy and is the symbol of the Palestinian national struggle.

What can creative diplomacy achieve in terms of a sustainable solution? Considering the value of Jerusalem to its constituencies, negotiations could conceivably continue forever. When an asset of such magnitude must be shared, a truly innovative and revolutionary effort is the only possibility for reaching a solution.

In view of the significance of the city to both peoples, a Pax Mediterraneo could include the following proposals: first, that the city of Jerusalem should remain as one city; and second, that the city of Jerusalem should have three political jurisdictions:

- **Yerushalayim** ("Jerusalem" in Hebrew) can be the capital of Israel and can include all Jewish neighborhoods and holy places, including the Western Wall.

- **Al-Quds** ("Jerusalem" in Arabic) can be the capital of Palestine and can include all Palestinian neighborhoods and Islamic holy places, including the surface of the Temple Mount and its mosques. The territory underneath the Temple Mount can be dealt with in coordination between the two sides.

- **Jerusalem** can be an area in the northwest of the city that enjoys joint UN, Israeli, and Palestinian jurisdiction. The United Nations can declare Jerusalem the world capital of peace. A quarter of UN institutions could be moved to Jerusalem, including the headquarters of the peacekeeping forces, UNESCO, and facilities for a temporary general assembly and secretary-general that will hold special sessions on peace-related topics at least once a year.

  UNESCO could promote cultural exchange and multiculturalism, with a clear mandate to foster a culture of peace in the world. Simultaneously, the move can make Jerusalem a major center for interfaith dialogue and understanding. Buildings can be designed by world-renowned architects. Jerusalem can finally be worthy of its name, the City of Peace.

Through the establishment of three jurisdictions, the inhabitants of Jerusalem and everyone emotionally linked to this unique city will benefit.

In 2001, I expressed these ideas to the leaderships of Israel, the Palestinian Authority, and the United Nations and found reactions on all sides to be encouraging. The plan would make Jerusalem the second-biggest UN headquarters and a center of peace in the context of a permanent status agreement. Jerusalem also would adhere to a new security dimension and regime when UN peacekeeping forces, with a bilateral agreement, are able to position peacekeepers in sensitive areas among both populations. Although the logistics of such an operation may seem overwhelming, it would demonstrate a great commitment to the ideals of modern peace and would prove how the tenets of creative diplomacy can be a driving force for peace and security.

The Golan Heights also will require a creative diplomatic solution, between Israel and Syria. It has become clear that peace will not reign in the Golan Heights without a full Israeli withdrawal from the strategic plateau that overlooks all of northern Israel. The exact border for withdrawal will require intense negotiations, because Israel will not allow Syria a foothold on the Sea of Galilee, Israel's main water resource. However, using innovative measures that necessarily involve a degree of mutual respect and trust on both sides, negotiations can be eased by making the Golan Heights a special demilitarized zone for eco- and health tourism. The region would fall under Syrian sovereignty, using Spanish, French, and Italian resources and infrastructure. Syrian residents and Israeli, Arab, and international tourists all can enjoy the benefits of such a proposal. Further proposals for the Golan Heights are presented later in this chapter.

A New View of Security

Creative diplomacy requires us to take a new look at what we consider "security." Instead of outlining the movements and limitations of each side's military as totally separate entities, modern security arrangements can focus on joint military programs that encourage cross-border cooperation and the recognition of common peacekeeping aims. Security arrangements can expand into the sociopolitical arena, where regional bodies can counsel and support cooperation on issues of borders, peacekeeping, terrorism, and crisis management.

Mediterranean Partnership for Peace

To provide a forum for security arrangements, Mediterranean nations can come together in a Mediterranean Partnership for Peace (MPFP) modeled on the Eastern European Partnership for Peace with NATO. Given the strategic importance of the Mediterranean—particularly the Middle East—for the United States, it can take the lead with NATO in this process. The United States can emphasize its regional function in its defense relationships with Palestine (antiterror cooperation), Jordan and Egypt (military assistance), and Syria (demilitarization of industries).

The special relationship between Israel and the United States can be similarly highlighted. A defense pact between the two can be created in light of Israel's withdrawal from most of the occupied territories and its location amid Arab nations. This pact could guarantee Israel's qualitative technological edge and security, aid its regional integration, and institutionalize existing and future relationships between Israel and the United States. This pact does not have to antagonize Israel's Arab neighbors if it ensures that the United States will remain an honest broker in the political domain, and particularly in the economic sphere, where it can provide much-needed assistance to the Arab world.

All sides will feel more secure if the Pax Mediterraneo is conceptually linked to a political-military model that broadens the scope of security elements to ensure that, in the case of a political breakdown, a military reprisal is not on the agenda. The MPFP—in line with the Eastern European pact—is just such a model.

Under the framework of the MPFP, NATO could sign individual partnership programs (IPPs) with the non-NATO Mediterranean countries that do not already have IPPs (Algeria, Bosnia and Herzegovina, Cyprus, Egypt, Israel, Jordan, Lebanon, Libya, Montenegro, Morocco, the Palestinian Authority, Serbia, Syria, and Tunisia).[3] Each IPP could entail military cooperation, peacekeeping arrangements, crisis management, civil emergency planning, politico-military dialogue, and transparency in national defense. Transparency in this context can involve parliamentary monitoring of public security and decision making in relation to potential security threats, territorial integrity, and political independence. Four Mediterranean countries—Albania, Macedonia, Malta, and Slovenia—already have IPPs with NATO. One of these countries, possibly Malta, can therefore serve as the central headquarters for MPFP activities.

Members of the MPFP can demonstrate their dedication to modern peace by signing a document committing signatories to preserve pluralist society; to preserve the principles of international law, the UN Charter (1945),[4] and the Universal Declaration of Human Rights; to refrain from the use of force, respect recognized borders, and settle disputes peacefully; and to fulfill existing obligations on disarmament and arms control. By establishing these common responsibilities, MPFP member countries can demonstrate solidarity and mutual trust.

Each member of the MPFP can appoint liaison officers to NATO. These officers can create a steering committee and working forum that link the new partners and NATO. These can operate in tandem with NATO's North Atlantic Council and coordinate issues relating to the IPPs. The North Atlantic Council can address political and security issues as well as cooperate on security-oriented economic questions, social issues, and matters of science and the environment. The steering committee also can deal with cooperative peacekeeping activities, providing a forum for consultation and exchange on political and conceptual issues of cooperation. The committee can report periodically to the North Atlantic Council and to MPFP foreign ministers.

Through a planning and review process, NATO can evaluate the capacity of each MPFP partner to participate in multinational training, exercises, and operations with the alliance. NATO and the new partners also can cooperate on civil and emergency training; humanitarian assistance and disaster procedures; scientific and environmental issues; military issues, including the conversion of military industries to civilian industries; and air traffic and maritime management.

The Mediterranean Partnership for Peace has the opportunity to reflect the objectives of a modern peace and to convert matters of security into civilian and political concepts. It can employ joint discussions and open dialogue to implement stability rather than leaving it a matter for the battlefield. Indeed, the MPFP embodies many of the concepts of modern peace: civil-military dialogue; democratization of national armed forces; transparency of budgets; an enhanced role of foreign ministers in relation to security issues; and scientific, environmental, and humanitarian coopera-tion in the defense arena. Security and defense arrangements can be approached from the perspective of peace and cooperation rather than as if to prepare for the next war.

This new approach would allow creative and sustainable frame-works for peace. Through the MPFP, for example, Syria and Israel can cooperate on military issues, ranging from monitoring to joint exercises to the exchange of military information, without the taint of "concessions." On a larger level, this partnership can create a strategic alliance with the West that will serve to democratize and civilize security.

Other security arrangements can include the establishment of an arms control committee. In this context, all nations should declare a vision for a nuclear-free Mediterranean (excepting France), conditioned on a nuclear-free Iran, to prevent a nonconventional weapons threat against any of the parties.

Similarly, regional cooperation in the struggle against terrorism is an important part of creating regional harmony and security. Mediterranean nations must pledge to fight terror, arrest terrorists, and dismantle terrorist infrastructure on their lands, and they must freeze international financing of terrorist organizations that gain passage through Mediterranean countries. Along these lines, reli-gious leaders can influence their constituents toward modern peace by endorsing such initiatives and denouncing the use of terror.

Mediterranean Peacekeeping and Peacebuilding Force

The security arrangements outlined in the Pax Mediterraneo can include the establishment of a multinational Mediterranean peacekeeping and peacebuilding force (MPPF). This force can be deployed in previously agreed-upon areas for monitoring purpos-es, taking its mandate from the UN Security Council. In the Middle East, the force can be positioned along the Israeli-Palestinian bor-der, the Palestinian-Egyptian border, the Israeli-Syrian border, and the Israeli-Lebanese border to monitor bilateral security arrangements and to ensure the demilitarization of the future Palestine (except for its internal police force). Israeli, Palestinian, and Jordanian security personnel can join the MPPF in the Jordan Valley and along the Palestinian side of the Jordan River (including at border crossings), to facilitate border crossings. This arrangement should last for a period of no less than six years, but it can be extended with the consent of both parties.

The MPPF also can extend its skills to peacebuilding activities. The Jordan Valley can be the location of MPPF peacebuilding activity in the areas of agriculture and water, while the Israeli-Palestinian border will house MPPF-facilitated industrial zones. Forces also can be deployed on the Golan Heights, on top of the mountain and along the new peace border, and along the Israeli-Lebanese border. According to the modern peace treaty, the region should be otherwise demilitarized, and Syria's standing army—as opposed to Israel's mainly reserve army—can be deployed a reasonable distance from the border to prevent a surprise attack against Israel. Some arrangements can be made with respect to the Israeli army—again, to prevent a surprise attack on Syrian troops.

In Lebanon, Hezbollah can be disarmed according to UN Security Council Resolutions 1559 (2004)[5] and 1701 (2006).[6] The MPPF can engage in peacebuilding activity in southern Lebanon and can monitor all security arrangements in the region, especially in light of the recent war. In a demonstration of cooperation and international support, the MPPF can be stationed in Jerusalem's UN headquarters, which can also administer special forces—only by consent of both parties—in the city's holy places. This deployment can serve to ensure public order and should be mostly symbolic in nature (i.e., light weapons only).

The creation of a Mediterranean peacekeeping and peacebuilding force is an innovative approach to long-standing security problems between Mediterranean countries. Implementing the MPPF and other nontraditional security arrangements will require a great deal of creativity and flexibility in the diplomatic process.

The Role of the International Community

The modern peace can be revolutionary—but only if it is given priority throughout the process and is not simply delayed until a treaty has been signed and a half-baked peace has been implemented. All the elements of peace—human rights, security, and the four pillars of modern peace—must be given equal political and financial footing during the peace process, both by the parties in conflict and by the international community. Within our Mediterranean context, the United Nations can deliberate the nature of peace, endorse the new peace deal, and guide the most effective implementation processes for governments within the conflict zone and in the larger region. In the event that a UN headquarters is established in Jerusalem (as is proposed in our creative diplomatic plan), these UN-Mediterranean discussions can take place in our world capital of peace.

Diplomacy that deals with peacebuilding, glocalization, and peace ecology can be subsidized by a financial mechanism established by the G-8. This mechanism could link Mediterranean partners, local governments, and local and international NGOs. Funding also can involve a Mediterranean regional bank that will assist in financing private-sector projects.

The role of the US administration in Mediterranean peace is critical. For this role to be executed effectively—that is, for the United States to show the true colors of its generosity and its genuine zeal for the gospel of democracy and the free market—the mind-set of both the administration and the American public needs to change. They must recognize and internalize the concept that peace is made by entrenching peace values within a local culture, not by forcing democracy and free market policies on societies so different from their own. Although both democracies and free market economies are desirable, peace should come first, bringing political and economic reforms in its wake. Furthermore, the United States must alter its security-oriented mind-set to take into account cultural perspectives that will stimulate economic development, cooperation, peacebuilding, and peace ecology in a given region. The US government can improve its image abroad and improve opportunities for American businesses by recognizing that peace—not force—is the best path to democracy.

But great change in the American mind-set will not come easily. There can be public recognition of and debate about the failures of conventional peacemaking and about the reforms necessary to cultivate a modern peace. These debates can happen on local, national, regional, and global levels and can involve peace workers from all walks of life. The Pax Mediterraneo is a good starting point for grounding the ideals of modern peace into a practical yet revolutionary peace plan. Ultimately, it is the United States, along with regional partners and international counterparts, that must lead the way to innovative peacemaking in conflict and post-conflict zones, by empowering local parties to implement a modern peace within their own cultural frameworks.

CONCLUSION

A New Vision for 2020

THE AMERICAN ESPOUSAL OF DEMOCRATIZATION AS A BASIS
for peace is not without merit. If the world comprised solely democratic countries, perhaps conflict and war would be less prevalent
and peace might triumph. Nonetheless, although democratization-
leads-to-peace theory looks good in textbooks, reality illuminates
its many flaws. Since 2001, when Gambia joined the democratic
club, democratic countries have represented 121 of 194 countries
worldwide.[1] However, of those 121 democracies, only 90 are liberal democracies that enjoy civil and political rights—hardly an
environment in which to cultivate lasting peace. And even "true"
democracies are not exempt from participation in war, as the United
States has demonstrated in Iraq and Afghanistan.

However noble the cause of democratization might be, it doesn't
hold true to the reality on the ground. Not only that, but its imposition conflicts with its essence. If we go to war to achieve peace,
we only perpetuate a cycle of violence. Almost all attempts to
impose democracy have been rejected—except in some individual
countries, such as in Germany and Japan after World War II. These
countries were successful in attaining democratic standards because
they had internal motivation for such a move. Democracy must
stem from the desires of the people; it cannot be imposed against
the wishes or culture of a society.

Besides, waiting for a global-democratic state of affairs is not
an option; we must take immediate action if we want to stop the
bloodshed and avert the possibility of an apocalyptic catastrophe.

This book has offered immediate, practical suggestions to end
war and nourish long-term peace—actions that don't require a

prerequisite imposition of democracy. Our modern peace, in fact, suggests the opposite: it is peace that must be a prerequisite for democracy, instead of the other way around. During times of conflict, societies have little incentive to encourage participatory democracy. In times of peace, however, societies are receptive to regional and international relationships that allow pluralist ideas to penetrate. Open borders translate into open economies, which in turn translate into cooperation, tolerance, and peace. Once peace is planted in a society, greater political and economic reforms—including democratic elements—can start to take root. Peace also will weaken the militant elements who object to openness.

Our modern peace, based on the four pillars of participatory peace and glocalization, peace ecology, peacebuilding, and creative democracy, is an attempt to create a model that can apply to *any* culture, identity, or political system. Ultimately, this approach to peace will lead to more open societies, regardless of the original environment. Many nondemocratic countries have signed peace agreements while remaining insular—Egypt and Jordan are two prime examples.

Our modern peace is not predicated on the existence of democratic elements within a society. Instead, it requires that we take a revolutionary approach to peacemaking, concentrating on the participation of grassroots groups and local governments rather than on rigid national bureaucracies. When peace is built from the ground up, its core will always be the citizen, not the politician, the economy, or the corporation. This citizens' peace will encourage the support and participation of the people, leading to the democratization of peace and contributing to greater openness, tolerance, and pluralism in the society and in the region.

In today's tense and often violent world, the fundamental human right to live almost demands an addendum: the right to live *in peace*. The freedom to achieve peace is more feasible than the transformation of a closed, nondemocratic society into a free and democratic one. External encouragement toward peace will not be perceived as a diktat; peace itself, rather than society, will be democratized—it will be placed in the hands of the people whose lives will be most affected.

In the introduction to this book, I presented a terrifying but realistic scenario for the year 2020, a scenario rooted in continued violence and hatred. That future, or something like it, almost certainly awaits us if we continue on our current path. We face a dire situation in the failure of traditional peacemaking methods, the declining power of central governments, the proliferation of nonconventional weapons of mass destruction, and the dangerous marriage of fundamentalist ideology with massive poverty. In addition, despite the evidence in support of participatory peace, governments typically are reluctant to change their basic approaches to peacemaking or to transfer powers to civil societies; in other words, governments are not prepared to let go of "state" issues to make them "people" issues. In light of these patterns, our current path looks difficult to change.

But I am an optimist by nature and an activist by profession. When, in the introduction, I acknowledged my distress over the global climate of conflict, I said I was not alone; neither am I alone in my optimism. In the course of writing this book, I reached out to a number of political leaders, thinkers, and artists—including five Nobel laureates—to hear their views on our current state of affairs and their hopes for the future.[2] In these final pages, I have collected their thoughts and prophecies for a new vision of the year 2020.

These are people who have struggled in the trenches of conflict, hatred, and violence—the worst of our time—and still blaze forth with hope and integrity. They are among the leaders prepared to take on the global challenges that must be overcome—particularly the increasing gap between rich and poor that so often gives rise to violent conflict. Their visions, presented here, underscore the need for a revolutionary peace that decentralizes the process and invites people from all walks of life to share in the fruits of peace.

Shimon Peres puts it this way:

Man is awakening at the dawn of this century with amazing possibilities at his disposal. Atomic bombs on the one hand and nanotechnology on the other. He can destroy worlds and he can build worlds. What will prevent destruction? And who will ensure growth?

Under no circumstances must artificial intelligence prevail over natural intelligence. Man must know more, yet he must also be aware of the one thing that forms the basis of his being: the difference between right and wrong. It is necessary to open borders, the skies, and minds. Science calls for democracy. It makes the lives of dictators hard.

Discrimination is not only a matter of age; it is also a matter of place. For instance, the world has turned its back on a whole continent—the African continent. This is a very serious error. Anyone who wants to prevent local famine from turning into global violence must understand that it is not sufficient to fight the manifestation of violence; it is also necessary to fight the reasons for the violence—namely, hunger, discrimination, ignorance. Learn how to know. Acquire an education and be able to discern right from wrong.

Mikhail Gorbachev cautions against the inherent contradictions of globalization and reiterates the need for cooperation:

The world is becoming less and less predictable. We have now created the breeding grounds for new wars. In these new times … one must renounce force as a decisive factor in world politics, and one must emphasize dialogue, negotiation, partnership, and cooperation. But if we continue to ignore or avoid these modern challenges, if we continue to proceed only from the practical

and in fact self-serving interests of this or that country
or group of countries, ignoring the interests of substantial portions of the world, then we risk losing again. We
risk wasting these first two decades of the new century
and not using them effectively to build a better world.

A correct assessment of current global processes pre-
cludes downplaying the role of the nation-state. Even
though this role is changing, national dignity and self-
awareness are still valid. However, this must not run
counter to regional and multilateral interests. The United
Nations should be both more democratic and proactive
in order to be able to keep the peace and maintain security at present levels, and to become an efficient guaran-
tor of rights and freedoms.

Nelson Mandela emphasizes humanity's common values and
calls for greater and more effective global governance:

Ordinary men and women all over the globe share the
simple wish to lead decent lives in conditions of stability
and basic comfort.... For global governance to succeed
in serving the ideals of universal peace, brother- and
sisterhood, and greater socioeconomic equality, it is
imperative that the functioning and integration of
regional and continental organizations be improved
and enhanced.

F. W. de Klerk, Mandela's partner in the South African peacemaking process, expands on Mandela's notion of an integrated
international governance and shares his hopes:

I remain optimistic. I believe that the world in which we
shall live in 2020 will be better than the world that we
know today. A greater percentage of the world's population will enjoy the benefits of freedom, prosperity, and

exciting new technologies. However, there is no room
for complacency. We will need to close the global gap
between rich and poor, because poverty is the breeding
ground for terrorism, tyranny, and conflict. We will need
to make the world safe for diversity—so that different
communities, countries, and regions will be able to
coexist peacefully ... [We] need to develop a global
culture of communal rights in the same way that we
have started to entrench acceptance of individual rights
... I believe that we will move toward a multitiered
order in which regional organizations, nation-states,
regions within countries, cities and schools and community boards all will play significant and balanced roles.

My negotiating partner Abu Ala firmly believes that the Israeli-
Palestinian conflict will be resolved; I find his conviction particularly inspiring:

In the coming two decades, the peoples of this region
will pour their energies into constructive actions, prosperity, law and order, justice, peace, and respect of
human rights. This is truth; a fact that I am confident
will reach fruition ... [I have] no doubt that our children will succeed in realizing the greatest prize, peace,
most definitely before the year 2020.

Former German chancellor Gerhard Schröder proposes the European model as a framework for solving regional conflicts worldwide:

The nation-state will almost certainly continue to be the
most important point of reference and of identity for
most people for a long time to come. However, it will
have to be integrated to an ever greater extent into
regional and worldwide cooperation.... I hope that
by 2020 other regions, too, will have found forms of

conflict settlement and reconciliation of interests similar
to those we have in Europe.

Quincy Jones, the legendary music producer who worked with
the Glocal Forum on We Are the Future (see chapter 3), emphasizes
the need for youth empowerment:

> It's in the eyes of children more than anything else that
> I find my motivation to work toward a better, more
> equitable future for all of them, everywhere. And it's
> in the eyes of children that I find my optimism about
> reaching that goal. I don't think the answer lies with
> governments, although surely many solutions require
> their participation. And while governments must embrace
> peace over war, I'm not convinced they will do this on
> their own, unless of course we nurture leaders of tomor-
> row, leaders of 2020, who have a strong and unshakable
> commitment to it.
>
> I believe it's the world citizenry who will nurture the
> global will to commit to a future where every child's
> eyes shine with energy, good health, curiosity, and the
> contentment that comes with being loved and safe.
> Indeed, they should be able to count on this as a God-
> given right.

Irish American writer Frank McCourt seconds the notion that
children are integral to the peacemaking process:

> An Israeli boy tells his parents of the exploits of a
> Palestinian boy on his soccer team. There is travel back
> and forth. A Palestinian girl studies Hebrew to under-
> stand her neighbors—or, perhaps, to marry one of them.
> Someday, and not so far off, these suffering people
> might challenge each other on the field of sports.

Actress Kathleen Turner believes in art as a crucial component of cultivating mutual understanding—in other words, she espouses the creation of a peace ecology:

> We experience art through our senses, and for that reason it helps us draw closer to others in a personal way. Art educates us, not only about our own experiences but also about those of other people, other cultures. Art transcends politics ... Therein lies our hope for peace and improved lives.

As for myself, although I feel vindicated by the views of these eminent leaders, I am more skeptical. My skepticism has inspired the words in this book; the revolutionary *Peace First* model stems from both realism about our current path and optimism about our ability to change it.

Of course, not all political leaders possess the humanitarian values and foresight of Nelson Mandela or Shimon Peres. Most continue on the traditional path in search of power, possessions, and prestige, denouncing decentralization and imposing their political will on the weak. The failings of such leaders is why reform at all levels—not only negotiations or peace treaties but also politics and international affairs—is integral to the modernization of peace.

It is my greatest hope that this book will lead to constructive and lively discussion about the nature of international relations and peacemaking in our modern era. We owe this to our youth, who in the year 2020 will be on their way to leading our nation-states. Kenya Jones (Quincy Jones's ten-year-old daughter) is a member of this crucially important generation. Her vision for 2020 echoes the passion and conviction of our greatest leaders:

> My dream for 2020 is no more homeless people. No more wars and fights but peace! More education. Not getting what you want but getting what you need. No

more killing people or animals or plants or trees. No
more pollution. No more crimes. No poor countries.
Everyone to share. Everyone's dreams to come true.

Ten or fifteen years down the line, these ideals may not have to
be translated into policy—they may exist in the minds and hearts
of each citizen. Ultimately, peace must exist on a personal level as
well as within the framework of the international community. We
must not be content to let our modern visionaries do all the work.
We must assume responsibility for cultivating peace in our own
lives and in our own spheres of influence, however large or small.
Revolutionizing peace is not one option—it is the *only* option.

From my perspective, at least, the concepts elucidated in these
pages have already begun to take root, not simply by virtue of their
publication but also as a result of my personal encounters during
the writing and production of this book. One such experience was
the Arabic publication of *Peace First*, the release of which closely
followed the book's original Hebrew publication in Israel.

Soon after the Arabic edition was published, I embarked on a
trip to visit my old friend and counterpart Abu Ala in his office in
Abu Dis, just next to Jerusalem. After negotiating the two Oslo
Accords, Abu Ala went on to be appointed as the second prime
minister of the Palestinian Authority, following the resignation of
Abu Mazen in 2003. He remains one of the prominent leaders of
the Palestinian Authority and its chief negotiator for permanent
peace.

To my great fortune, our association in Oslo has transcended
the political arena and we continue to enjoy a close and dynamic relationship. I suppose that at some point, after years of heated
debate and "fighting" around the negotiating table, we developed a
deep personal affinity for each other—becoming the best of friends
and the most former of enemies. As representatives of two rival
peoples embroiled in conflict, we took a leap of faith that continues to bind us tightly together.

And so it was with much excitement that I went to visit Abu Ala, holding in my hands a signed copy of the Arabic version of *Peace First,* fresh off the press.

As always, we continue to "negotiate" when we meet. Old habits die hard, and old friendships die harder. We spoke about the conditions of permanent peace between our two peoples and intuited that our positions were remarkably not too far apart. It was clear to both of us that permanent peace borders must be based primarily on the 1967 lines, allowing for land swaps and modest modifications that enable Israel to incorporate three to four settlement blocs into sovereign Israel and to remove Jewish settlements from most of the West Bank.

Our views were also quite close on the loaded question of Jerusalem. Ultimately, Arab and Jewish neighborhoods shall be governed by the Palestinians and Israelis, respectively. Even on the intractable issue of refugees, Abu Ala understood, like other Palestinian leaders, that notwithstanding the principle of the right of return, to which he adheres, Israel would not commit demographic suicide by allowing a large influx of Palestinian refugees within its sovereign borders. We also echoed common sentiments regarding the need to combat terrorism and to uphold security for both populations through cooperation, and perhaps through the involvement of international monitoring. Yet most importantly, we agreed that peace must be based on the active support of both peoples. What we both understood—somewhat ironically—was that peace cannot be fostered merely between politicians, that it needs to be created as a modern peace between peoples.

Finally, the moment had come for me to present Abu Ala with the Arabic edition of *Peace First.* When I placed it on the table before him he gave me a mischievous look and, to my astonishment, said that he had already read it, or at least the first few chapters of it.

"Impossible!" I retorted. I told him the book in my hands was the very first copy of the Arabic version. It had arrived from Amman only the day before. But before I had even finished my explanation, Abu Ala tauntingly waved a copy of that day's *Al-Quds* at me. He laughed and explained that *Al-Quds,* the leading Palestinian daily newspaper, had already published four chapters of my book.

I was flabbergasted. Of course, I had known that *Al-Quds* was considering publishing an article about the book, but I could not have dreamed that it would publish four chapters in their entirety prior to the release of the Arabic edition. Ultimately, they—along with a Kuwaiti newspaper, *Al-Rai Al-Aam*—published the entire book, cover to cover. Other Arabic media (including Egyptian, Jordanian, Lebanese, Qatari, and Saudi press) offered positive reviews of the book after the 2008 Cairo Book Fair, an act that represented a compelling statement and a powerful step toward peace.

My personal experience that day with Abu Ala served as a timely example of the four pillars of my thesis. Participatory peace and glocalization were apparent in the groundbreaking publication of an Israeli peace book in a city newspaper, and its appearance in virtually every Palestinian home in the West Bank offered a direct line to citizens. Peacebuilding was exemplified in this cross-border exchange of knowledge for mutual benefit, and the media's support of a campaign of peace and coexistence was a good example of peace ecology. Finally, I felt as though my dialogue with Abu Ala and our mutual openness to lateral thinking was a testament to the principle of creative diplomacy.

To further bolster my sense of optimism, Abu Ala presented me with two pages he had written about his connection with the book, to which he was an important symbolic contributor. Those pages—representing a political statement as well as a statement of peace—have become the afterword of this English edition.

For an Israeli peace publication to have the support of a leading figure in the Palestinian Authority is at the very least a symbolic step toward the realization of modern peace; it is a sign that even in the most complicated and dire of conflicts, hope is not lost. And so I left Abu Ala's offices in Abu Dis with the unwavering belief that a modernized peace process is not only an imperative but also a realistic and viable pursuit. We must not be dissuaded by the fear of war, nor by the fear of cooperation. Peace in our world is possible, and it is our great privilege and responsibility to usher it in.

AFTERWORD

by Abu Ala (Ahmed Qurei)

WHEN I FIRST MET URI SAVIR IN OSLO, HE HAD A NOTICEABLE personality that distinguished him from the other members of the Israeli delegation. His was a character of conviction and integrity, a personality that contributed immensely to a new phase of the relations between Israelis and Palestinians. Throughout the negotiations, Uri maintained absolute belief in the importance of the realization of the peace process; he continued defending and persevering in the spread of his vision, even in the face of difficult opposition. Uri distanced himself from the pretexts, prejudices, and artificial allegations that inevitably aim to stop the course of the peace process—thus proving his complete commitment to peace, and laying the foundations for the peacemaking model that would later develop into this book.

My relationship with Uri Savir has not waned since our first encounter fifteen years ago, when our professional interaction became infused with friendship—not even after Uri quit his official position. The achievement that we created together in Oslo has remained a warm memory as a peace process that was filled with hope; it was the start of a new page in the history of the interlaced relations between two neighboring peoples. These relations later stumbled, facing a series of cruel failures, but they did not fall. The historic agreement at Oslo was the only political caretaker for the developments that took place afterward, and the foundation for the accomplishments our people have achieved.

Uri may have quit his office, but he has not quit his mission as a permanent ambassador for peacemaking. He unites theory and practice in his life and in his work. *Peace First* is distinguished by a great intellectual effort, by writing that stems from a deep historical understanding and from Uri's personal involvement as a peacemaker in many regional and internal conflicts. Uri has shared his knowledge and experience with great eloquence, placing historical precedents and examples in a philosophical framework that enriches his overall message of passion and pragmatism. This book emphasizes peace as the conscious human response to the social, economic, and security challenges that states, institutions, and individuals all face, especially during this era of the global village.

Much of today's peacemaking is characterized by a rush of assistance from the international community and its penetrating powers. Uri's approach—cultivating peace within a framework of cooperation, creative diplomacy, and common values—invites a broad group of peacemakers into the process, including governments, businesses, and nongovernmental organizations. I consider this socially inclusive approach to be the best and only way to achieve modern peace.

Uri's model, as set out in *Peace First,* is an appropriate manual for settling peace in the world and in our region, taking into consideration the particularity of the Palestinian-Israeli conflict and the amount of suspicion and inherited hostility that exists. Both sides must continue to build peace that is based on the mutual conviction that peace is the people's ultimate choice. Or, as Uri says, peace is the people's first choice.

Through *Peace First,* Uri Savir proves that he is one of the chief stewards of the temple of peace. He continues to fulfill his duties with great perseverance, and he dedicates his intellectual life to finding solutions to conflict and unearthing the origins of the idea that tyrannizes him—peace.

Our region—our world—paces before the gates of peace but refrains from stepping over its threshold. We do not lack motivation or interest, but we suffer from a dearth of inspiring peace leaders such as Yasser Arafat and Yitzhak Rabin, and of faithful and devout people—peace bureaucrats—to initiate peace on the ground. If there were more people like Uri Savir to transform peace from creative and promising ideas to practical and tangible facts, we could move beyond empty rhetoric and toward action.

Every citizen has the potential to be a peacemaker, in the Middle East and across the world. Let us take Uri's message into our hearts and rise to the great responsibility before us, of revolutionizing the peacemaking process toward lasting, participatory, and modern peace.

NOTES

INTRODUCTION

1. Heidelberg Institute for International Conflict Research, *Conflict Barometer 2007*, http://www.hiik.de/konfliktbarometer/index.html.en (accessed April 10, 2008).
2. United States Institute of Peace, Peace Agreements Digital Collection, http://www.usip.org/library/pa.html (accessed January 22, 2008).
3. Nobel Foundation, "All Nobel Prize Laureates," http://nobelprize.org/nobel_prizes/peace/laureates (accessed January 22, 2008).
4. P. Stålenheim, C. Perdomo, and E. Sköns, *SIPRI Yearbook 2007* (New York: Oxford University Press, 2007), pp. 267–297.

CHAPTER 1. OLD-FASHIONED PEACEMAKING

1. "Chickasaw Treaty," 1805, available from the Avalon Project at Yale Law School, Yale University, http://www.yale.edu/lawweb/avalon/ntreaty/nt003.htm (accessed January 22, 2008).
2. "Treaties with the Barbary Powers," 1786–1836, available from the Avalon Project at Yale Law School, Yale University, http://www.yale.edu/lawweb/avalon/diplomacy/barbary/barmenu.htm (accessed January 22, 2008).
3. Eric Hobsbawm, *The Age of Extremes: A History of the World, 1914–1991* (New York: Vintage, 1994).
4. "Versailles Treaty," June 28, 1919, available from the Avalon Project at Yale Law School, Yale University, http://www.yale.edu/lawweb/avalon/imt/menu.htm (accessed January 22, 2008).
5. "North Atlantic Treaty," April 4, 1949, available from the Avalon Project at Yale Law School, Yale University, http://www.yale.edu/lawweb/avalon/nato.htm (accessed January 22, 2008).
6. US State Department's Bureau of International Information Programs, "The Marshall Plan (1947)," http://usinfo.state.gov/special/Archive/2005/Apr/29-923823.html (accessed January 22, 2008).
7. Islamicpopulation.com, "European Muslim Population," http://www.islamicpopulation.com/europe_general.html (accessed January 22, 2008).

8. Manav Tanneeru, "Inside the Hispanic Vote: Growing in Numbers, Growing in Diversity," CNN, September 28, 2007, http://www.cnn.com/2007/US/09/28/hispanic.vote/index.html (accessed January 22, 2008).

9. Heidelberg Institute for International Conflict Research, *Conflict Barometer 2007*, http://www.hiik.de/konfliktbarometer/index.html.en (accessed April 10, 2008).

10. "Dayton Peace Accords," 1995, available from the Avalon Project at Yale Law School, Yale University, http://www.yale.edu/lawweb/avalon/intdip/bosnia/daymenu.htm (accessed January 22, 2008).

11. Political Economy Research Institute, "Modern Conflicts Database: Alternative Estimates for Death Tolls," available from the University of Massachusetts Amherst, http://www.peri.umass.edu/fileadmin/pdf/dpe/modern_conflicts/death_tolls.pdf (accessed April 9, 2008).

12. "Peace Treaty and Principles of Interrelation between Russian Federation and Chechen Republic Ichkeria," May 12, 1997, available from Incore: International Conflict Research, http://www.incore.ulst.ac.uk/services/cds/agreements/casia.html (accessed January 22, 2008).

13. "Khasavyourt Joint Declaration and Principles for Mutual Relations," August 31, 1996, available from Incore: International Conflict Research, http://www.incore.ulst.ac.uk/services/cds/agreements/casia.html (accessed January 22, 2008).

14. "Agreement on a Firm and Lasting Peace," December 29, 1996, available from Incore: International Conflict Research, http://www.incore.ulst.ac.uk/services/cds/agreements/latin.html (accessed January 22, 2008).

15. Political Economy Research Institute, "Modern Conflicts Database: Alternative Estimates for Death Tolls," available from the University of Massachusetts Amherst, http://www.peri.umass.edu/fileadmin/pdf/dpe/modern_conflicts/death_tolls.pdf (accessed April 9, 2008).

16. Political Economy Research Institute, "Modern Conflicts Database: Alternative Estimates for Death Tolls," available from the University of Massachusetts Amherst, http://www.peri.umass.edu/fileadmin/pdf/dpe/modern_conflicts/death_tolls.pdf (accessed April 9, 2008).

17. "Peace Agreement between the Government of Sierra Leone and the Revolutionary United Front of Sierra Leone," July 7, 1999, available from the United States Institute of Peace, http://www.usip.org/library/pa/sl/sierra_leone_07071999.html (accessed January 22, 2008).

18. "Peace Agreement between the Government of Sudan and South Sudan United Democratic Salvation Front (UDSF)," April 21, 1997, available from Incore: International Conflict Research, http://www.incore.ulst.ac.uk/services/cds/agreements/africa.html (accessed April 7, 2008).

19. "The Northern Ireland Peace Agreement," April 10, 1998, available from the United States Institute of Peace, http://www.usip.org/library/pa/ni/nitoc .html (accessed January 22, 2008).

20. "Peace Treaty and Principles of Interrelation between Russian Federation and Chechen Republic Ichkeria," May 12, 1997, available from Incore: International Conflict Research, http://www.incore.ulst.ac.uk/services/cds/ agreements/casia.html (accessed January 22, 2008).

21. Ruth Gidley, "Crisis Profile: Death and Displacement in Chechnya," Reuters AlertNet, November 8, 2005, http://www.alertnet.org/thefacts/ reliefresources/111997274494.htm (accessed April 9, 2008).

22. "Peace Agreement between the Government of Sierra Leone and the Revolutionary United Front," July 7, 1999, available from the United States Institute of Peace, http://www.usip.org/library/pa/sl/sierra_leone_07071999 .html (accessed January 22, 2008).

23. UN High Commissioner for Refugees, as quoted in "Guatemala: Global IDP Figures" by the Internal Displacement Monitoring Centre, http://www .internal-displacement.org/idmc/website/countries.nsf/(httpEnvelopes)/ EE4DEA6CC40B5692802570B8005A7316?OpenDocument (accessed January 22, 2008).

24. United States Institute of Peace, "Truth Commissions Digital Collection," http://www.usip.org/library/truth.html#guatemala (accessed January 22, 2008).

CHAPTER 2. THE OSLO ROLLER COASTER: A MIXED MODEL

1. "Israel-Palestine Liberation Organization Agreement," September 13, 1993, available from the Avalon Project at Yale Law School, Yale University, http://www.yale.edu/lawweb/avalon/mideast/isrplo.htm (accessed March 27, 2008).

2. "The Israeli-Palestinian Interim Agreement on the West Bank and Gaza Strip," September 28, 1995, available from the Israeli Ministry of Foreign Affairs, http://www.israel.org/MFA/Peace%20Process/Guide%20to %20the%20Peace%20Process/THE%20ISRAELI-PALESTINIAN %20INTERIM%20AGREEMENT (accessed March 27, 2008).

3. Taylor and Francis Group, *The Middle East and North Africa 2003*, 49th edition (London: Europa Publications, 2002), p. 598.

4. "Reactions to Arafat's Reference to Jihad and Jerusalem," May 17, 1994, available from the Israel Ministry of Foreign Affairs, http://www.mfa.gov.il/ MFA/Archive/Speeches/REACTIONS%20TO%20ARAFAT-S %20REFERENCE%20TO%20JIHAD%20AND%20JERUS (accessed April 7, 2008).

5. "Agreement on the Gaza Strip and the Jericho Area," May 4, 1994, available from the Jewish Virtual Library, http://www.jewishvirtuallibrary.org/jsource/Peace/gazajer.html (accessed January 22, 2008).

6. "Gaza-Jericho Agreement Annex IV: Protocol on Economic Relations between the Government of the State of Israel and the PLO, Representing the Palestinian People," April 29, 1994, available from the Israel Ministry of Foreign Affairs, http://www.mfa.gov.il/MFA/Peace%20Process/Guide%20to%20the%20Peace%20Process/Gaza-Jericho%20Agreement%20Annex%20IV%20-%20Economic%20Protoco (accessed January 22, 2008).

7. World Bank and UN data.

8. BBC, "Jewish Settler Kills 30 at Holy Site," February 25, 1994, available from the BBC News archive, http://news.bbc.co.uk/onthisday/hi/dates/stories/february/25/newsid_4167000/4167929.stm (accessed January 22, 2008).

9. Clyde Haberman, "Israeli Ministers Debate Evictions of Jews in Hebron," *New York Times*, March 7, 1994, http://query.nytimes.com/gst/fullpage.html?res=9C00E5D61E3AF934A35750C0A962958260&sec=&spon=&pagewanted=all (accessed January 22, 2008).

CHAPTER 3. PARTICIPATORY PEACE AND GLOCALIZATION

1. Political Economy Research Institute, "Modern Conflicts Database: Alternative Estimates for Death Tolls," available from the University of Massachusetts Amherst, http://www.peri.umass.edu/fileadmin/pdf/dpe/modern_conflicts/death_tolls.pdf (accessed April 9, 2008).

2. United Nations Development Programme, "Human Development Report 2007/2008, 10: Survival: Progress and Setbacks, Infant Mortality Rate," http://hdrstats.undp.org/indicators/91.html (accessed April 9, 2008).

3. Human Rights Watch, "Child Soldiers," http://www.hrw.org/campaigns/crp/index.htm (accessed January 22, 2008).

4. World Bank, "World Development Indicators 2007," http://web.worldbank.org/WBSITE/EXTERNAL/DATASTATISTICS/0,,contentMDK:21298138~pagePK:64133150~piPK:64133175~theSitePK:239419,00.html (accessed April 9, 2008).

5. Charlotte Denny, "Cows are Better Off than Half the World," *The Guardian,* August 22, 2002, http://www.guardian.co.uk/worldsummit2002/earth/story/0,,777663,00.html (accessed April 9, 2008).

6. United Nations Development Programme, "Human Development Report 2007/2008, 6: Commitment to Health: Resources, Access and Services,

Health Expenditure Per Capita," http://hdrstats.undp.org/indicators/52 .html (accessed April 9, 2008).

7. World Bank, "World Development Indicators 2007," http://web.worldbank .org/WBSITE/EXTERNAL/DATASTATISTICS/0,,contentMDK:21298138 ~pagePK:64133150~piPK:64133175~theSitePK:239419,00.html (accessed April 9, 2008).

8. C. J. L. Murray, G. King, A. D. Lopez, N. Tomijima, and E. G. Krug, "Armed Conflict as a Public Health Problem," *British Medical Journal,* February 9, 2002, 324 (7333), pp. 346–349.

9. World Bank, Development Education Program, http://www.worldbank.org/ depweb/english/modules/economic/gnp/print.html (accessed January 22, 2008).

10. Pew Global Attitudes Project, "America Admired, Yet Its New Vulnerability Seen as Good Thing, Say Opinion Leaders," 2003, http://pewglobal.org/ reports/display.php?PageID=58 (accessed January 22, 2008).

11. UN-Habitat, "Urbanization: Facts and Figures," http://ww2.unhabitat.org/ istanbul+5/back11.doc (accessed April 9, 2008).

12. UN-Habitat, "State of the World's Cities 2006/7," http://www.unhabitat .org/content.asp?cid=3397&catid=7&typeid=46&subMenuId=0 (accessed April 9, 2008).

13. CERFE and Glocal Forum, "City to City Cooperation Cost-Effectiveness," June 2005, www.glocalforum.org/mediagallery/mediaDownload.php?mm=/ warehouse/documents/c2cce.pdf (accessed April 9, 2008).

14. Tamela Hultman, "Africa: Rome Concert Launches a Movement, Says Quincy Jones," May 19, 2004, http://allafrica.com/stories/200405190001 .html (accessed January 22, 2008).

CHAPTER 5. PEACEBUILDING

1. Alessandra Sulzer, "The Business of Cooperation: Peace and Profit through Joint Ventures," *Harvard International Review* 23 (Summer 2001), http:// www.harvardir.org/articles/912/1/ (accessed January 22, 2008).

CHAPTER 6. CREATIVE DIPLOMACY

1. Quoted in Ned Hermann, *The Whole Brain Business Book* (New York: McGraw Hill Professional, 1996).

CHAPTER 7. THE PEACE BAROMETER

1. Andrew C. Revkin, "A New Measure of Well-Being from a Happy Little Kingdom," *New York Times,* October 4, 2005, http://www.nytimes. com/2005/10/04/science/04happ.html?pagewanted=all (accessed January 22, 2008).

CHAPTER 8. PEACEMAKERS

1. Nissan Oren, *Anatomy of Leadership* (Israel: Hebrew University of Jerusalem, 1974).
2. Sarah Anderson and John Cavanagh, "Report on the Top 200 Corporations," Institute for Policy Studies, December 2000, summary at http://www.corporations.org/system/top100.html (accessed January 22, 2008).

CHAPTER 10. NEGOTIATION

1. Jan Steinbeck, one of Sweden's most famous and brilliant entrepreneurs, created a global media and telecommunications empire. I cofounded the Glocal Forum with Jan to advance intercity relations. Tragically, he passed away in 2002.

CHAPTER 11. THE PEACE TREATY

1. "General Peace Agreement for Mozambique," October 18, 1991, available from the United States Institute of Peace, http://www.usip.org/library/pa/mozambique/mozambique_11131991_p2.html#p2-01 (accessed January 29, 2008).
2. Fred Kaplan, "Who Disbanded the Iraqi Army?," *Slate,* September 7, 2007, http://www.slate.com/id/2173554/ (accessed January 22, 2008).

CHAPTER 14. PEACE IN THE MEDITERRANEAN BASIN: WHAT WILL IT TAKE?

1. Diogenes Laertius, *The Lives and Opinions of Eminent Philosophers,* trans. C. D. Yonge (London: Henry G. Bohn, 1853), available from Peitho's Web, http://www.classicpersuasion.org/pw/diogenes/dldiogenes.htm#cite (accessed January 22, 2008).
2. Abdelwahad Biad, "A Strategy for Conflict Prevention and Management in the Mediterranean," *Journal of CIDOB International Affairs 37: Stability and Conflict in the Mediterranean,* 1999.

CHAPTER 15. CITIES AND YOUTH

1. "Memorandum of Understanding," 2005, available from the Glocal Forum, http://glocalforum.existhost.com/gf/New_Glocal_Website/downloads/MOU_GlocalForum_World%20Bank.pdf (accessed April 9, 2008).
2. UNESCO World Heritage Centre, "World Heritage List," 2006, http://whc.unesco.org/en/list (accessed January 22, 2008).

CHAPTER 16. HUMAN RIGHTS AND PEACE EDUCATION

1. "Universal Declaration of Human Rights," December 1948, available from the United Nations, http://www.un.org/Overview/rights.html (accessed January 22, 2008).

CHAPTER 17. JOINT ECONOMIC, SOCIAL, ENVIRONMENTAL, AND TOURISM VENTURES

1. Central Intelligence Agency, *The World Factbook,* 2006–2007, https://www.cia.gov/library/publications/the-world-factbook/index.html (accessed January 22, 2008).

2. "Convention for the Protection of the Mediterranean Sea against Pollution," February 16, 1976, available from the United Nations Environmental Programme, http://www.unep.ch/regionalseas/regions/med/t_barcel.htm (accessed January 22, 2008).

3. Jennifer LeClaire, "Former NASA Chief Architect Brad Hines on Solar Power's Comeback," *Technology News Online,* November 24, 2006, http://www.technewsworld.com/story/54375.html (accessed January 22, 2008).

4. "Hydrogen Fuel: Information about Hydrogen Fuel Cell Technology," *Alternative Energy News,* http://www.alternative-energy-news.info/technology/hydrogen-fuel (accessed January 22, 2008).

5. David Faiman, "Solar Energy for the Promotion of Stability in the Mediterranean Basin" (Tel Aviv: Peres Center for Peace, 2005).

6. Moti Kaplan, "The Mediterranean Environment Situation and Principles for Sustainable Development: Regional and Environmental Planning" (Tel Aviv: Peres Center for Peace, 2005).

7. For more information, see the United Nations Environment Programme Mediterranean Action Plan Web site, http://www.unepmap.org (accessed January 22, 2008).

8. For more information, see the Euro-Mediterranean Partnership Web site, http://ec.europa.eu/external_relations/euromed/index.htm (accessed January 22, 2008).

CHAPTER 18. BORDERS, SECURITY, AND THE INTERNATIONAL COMMUNITY

1. "United Nations Security Council Resolutions Relating to the Middle East," available from the Avalon Project at Yale Law School, Yale University, http://www.yale.edu/lawweb/avalon/un/unres.htm (accessed March 27, 2008).

2. Foundation for Middle East Peace, "Jerusalem's Population, 1967–2003," *Report on Israeli Settlement in the Occupied Territories* 15 (March–April 2005), http://www.fmep.org/settlement_info/stats_data/jerusalem/jerusalems_population_1967-2003.html (accessed January 22, 2008).

3. "Signatures of Partnership for Peace Framework Document," available from the North Atlantic Treaty Organization, http://www.nato.int/pfp/sig-cntr.htm (accessed January 22, 2008).

4. "Charter of the United Nations," June 26, 1945, available from the United Nations, http://www.un.org/aboutun/charter (accessed March 27, 2008).

5. "UN Security Council Resolutions," available from the United Nations, http://www.un.org/Docs/sc/unsc_resolutions04.html (accessed March 27, 2008).

6. "UN Security Council Resolution 1701," available from the United Nations, http://www.un.org/Docs/journal/asp/ws.asp?m=s/res/1701(2006) (accessed March 27, 2008).

CONCLUSION: A NEW VISION FOR 2020

1. Freedom House, "Freedom in the World 2008: Selected Data from Freedom House's Annual Global Survey of Political Rights and Civil Liberties," http://www.freedomhouse.org/template.cfm?page=70&release=612 (accessed January 22, 2008).

2. Peres Center for Peace, 2020 Visions of the Future (Tel Aviv: Author, 2005).

ACKNOWLEDGMENTS

FIRST, I WANT TO THANK MY DEAR WIFE, ALIZA, WHO—TO-gether with our daughter, Maya—encouraged me to write this book.

I want to convey my gratitude to those who assisted me in the Israeli edition of my book: Ronit Zimmer from the Peres Center for Peace and Megan Hallahan from the Glocal Forum; Ronit Levy from Globus Translations; Maya Tal-Magen from the Peres Center for Peace, for an excellent editing job of the Hebrew version; and Inbal Yohanan from the Peres Center for Peace, for helping with marketing in the various languages. I also want to thank Yedioth Ahronoth Books and Chemed Books for the Israeli edition, Jalil Publications for the Arabic edition, and Luca Sossella Editore for the Italian edition. Thank you to Carmina, the lovely cafe in Tel Aviv that hosted me as I wrote this book.

I want to thank the entire excellent staff of Berrett-Koehler Publishers for the English edition of the book, especially Johanna Vondeling, editorial director; the marketing and publicity department; and Jenny Williams, the developmental editor for this project. I also would like to express my gratitude to Jeremie Bracka at the Peres Center for Peace for working with me on the English edition.

Additional thanks to my friends and colleagues at the Peres Center for Peace and the Glocal Forum for their amazing cooperation in peacebuilding; your inspiration was a guiding light for this book.

I want to thank my two friends and colleagues Dennis Ross and Abu Ala for the foreword and afterword, respectively. They are both brilliant and true peacemakers and humanists.

And last but not least, Shimon Peres—I had the honor to be inspired by this unique individual, Israel's man of peace. Thank you.

INDEX

ABOUT THE AUTHOR

URI SAVIR, ONE OF ISRAEL'S MOST SENIOR DIPLOMATS, WAS Israel's chief negotiator during the Oslo Accords between Israel and the Palestine Liberation Organization, between 1993 and 1996. In his role as director-general of the Israeli Foreign Ministry, he also negotiated with Jordan, with Syria, and in the multinational peace tracks in the Middle East. Prior to this, Savir was Israel's consul-general to New York and held various diplomatic positions in North America.

Savir is a graduate of the International Relations department of the Hebrew University in Jerusalem. He has worked for twenty-five years beside his mentor, Israel's current president, Shimon Peres. In 1996, Peres and Savir cofounded the Peres Center for Peace. In 1999, Savir was elected to the Knesset (Israeli parliament), where he served as the chair of the Subcommittee for Foreign Relations in the Defense and Foreign Relations Committee.

In 2001, after resigning from political life, Savir established the Glocal Forum, an Italy-based nongovernmental organization dealing with intercity relations in favor of peace and development. Simultaneously, he served on the board and was acting chairman of the largest free-sheet newspaper in the world, *Metro International*.

He is husband to Dr. Aliza Savir, father of the author Maya Savir, and grandfather to four. He is the author of the *New York Times* Notable Book *The Process: 1,100 Days That Changed the Middle East*.

About Berrett-Koehler Publishers

Berrett-Koehler is an independent publisher dedicated to an ambitious mission: Creating a World That Works for All.

We believe that to truly create a better world, action is needed at all levels—individual, organizational, and societal. At the individual level, our publications help people align their lives with their values and with their aspirations for a better world. At the organizational level, our publications promote progressive leadership and management practices, socially responsible approaches to business, and humane and effective organizations. At the societal level, our publications advance social and economic justice, shared prosperity, sustainability, and new solutions to national and global issues.

A major theme of our publications is "Opening Up New Space." They challenge conventional thinking, introduce new ideas, and foster positive change. Their common quest is changing the underlying beliefs, mindsets, and structures that keep generating the same cycles of problems, no matter who our leaders are or what improvement programs we adopt.

We strive to practice what we preach—to operate our publishing company in line with the ideas in our books. At the core of our approach is *stewardship,* which we define as a deep sense of responsibility to administer the company for the benefit of all of our "stakeholder" groups: authors, customers, employees, investors, service providers, and the communities and environment around us.

We are grateful to the thousands of readers, authors, and other friends of the company who consider themselves to be part of the "BK Community." We hope that you, too, will join us in our mission.

A BK Currents Book

This book is part of our BK Currents series. BK Currents books advance social and economic justice by exploring the critical intersections between business and society. Offering a unique combination of thoughtful analysis and progressive alternatives, BK Currents books promote positive change at the national and global levels. To find out more, visit www.bkcurrents.com.

Be Connected